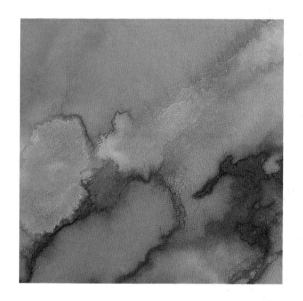

"After a time

the land is not

outside you,

but a part of where

you deeply breathe..."

Robin Skelton from "The Land"

WELCOME ABOARD

It is with great pleasure that VIA Rail™ welcomes you aboard. For no matter which route you choose from among the four described in this book, your journey will provide fascinating experiences and reveal stunning scenery.

The landscape slides by, punctuated now and then by many villages and communities. The rhythm of the passing miles soothes your psyche; you have time to reflect and leave the pressures of daily life behind. This is the world of train travel – a world where the excitement of travel is preserved and the traveller is awakened with the spirit of adventure. Trains are the visitor's passport to a country's colourful life and a richly rewarding way to enjoy the sights.

Enchanting Horizons is the title of this book, and it sets the stage for one of the world's most intriguing lands.

Seeing Western Canada by rail is like looking through a kaleidoscope, each view enhanced by the movement of the train. Depending on the season and the time of day, passing scenes will present themselves in their fullest glory.

Enchanting Horizons will complement your personal experience of riding the *Canadian* between Toronto and Vancouver, the *Skeena* between Jasper, Alberta and Prince Rupert on the west coast, the *Hudson Bay* between Winnipeg and Churchill, Manitoba and the *Malahat* on its historic day-route on Vancouver Island.

We hope you enjoy Enchanting Horizons. A wealth of additional information about scheduling, services and dining may be obtained from VIA Rail personnel, and our staff will be pleased to share their knowledge of the routes and help identify landmarks. Their boundless enthusiasm adds another dimension to your experience.

ALL ABOARD!

From the moment you board the train, it's easy to understand that you are departing on a special journey. Each traveller directs his or her own adventure, with moments to gaze out the windows, capture a scene or event on camera or strike up a friendship with a fellow passenger. Each train's interior provides a satisfying environment, with plenty of room to move about. Also, on some trains, private spaces for reading and contemplation, lounges and dining facilities are available.

We at VIA™ wish you a wonderful journey. Sit back, relax and enjoy.

VIA PLEASES ALL PASSENGERS

The *Canadian* and the *Skeena* trains are easily recognized by their gleaming stainless steel cars, while the *Malahat* features RDC (rail diesel car) trains and the *Hudson Bay* uses conventional equipment. Both the *Skeena* and *Hudson Bay* offer Coach Class and sleeping car accommodations.

The stainless steel cars of the *Canadian* and the *Skeena* were put into service in 1955. They've been completely restored, offering elegance in an art-deco style that's been enhanced by graceful etched glass and original Canadian artwork throughout. The colour scheme adds another dimension, using the jades, pinks and grays that will be seen in the landscape of Canada.

Two types of service are available on the *Canadian,* and both provide comfort and excellent service: *Silver and Blue*™ Class and Coach Class.

Silver and Blue Class passengers will enjoy Sleeping cars that have a shower in each car, panoramic views from the Domed Observatory, the intimacy of the Mural Lounge and the wrap-around windows of the uniquely shaped Bullet Lounge. Superb service and gourmet meals are provided in the Dining car.

And for Coach Class passengers, there are ultra-comfortable seats as well as a Skyline car, with a dome, lounge, snack bar and café.

A BIT OF HISTORY

Canada's first national link was forged by the Canadian Pacific Railway from 1881-1885. The tracks reached from the eastern cities, across the rugged Canadian Shield north of the Great Lakes, across the Prairies and through

the mountain passes of the Rockies.

The Great Northern Railway (1896-1917) and the Grand Trunk Pacific (1902-1923) laid track across the Canadian north, and later amalgamated as the publicly owned Canadian National Railway.

Both the Canadian Pacific and Canadian National had freight and passenger networks, and in 1978 their passenger networks were united as VIA Rail Canada. From the beginning, VIA has been committed to rewarding passengers with quality service and comfort.

HOW TO USE THIS BOOK

This guide has four colour-coded sections for the four routes followed by the *Canadian, Skeena, Hudson Bay* and *Malahat.* Each section contains an introduction to the route, overviews of the provinces or regions crossed, profiles of major cities and a guide to the sights along the way. Maps of the trains' routes are placed in proximity to the accompanying text.

One of the railway traditions – the milepost – provides the key to locating a train's current position. Though Canada now uses the metric system, the original markers for railroads were, and still are, in miles. Each line is subdivided at *Railway Division Points;* these subdivisions are not a standard length, they were based on the distance a steam locomotive could travel in a day. The miles are counted from '0' going east to west, or south to north.

Mileposts may be on either side of a train, and are usually rectangular white signs with black numbers. On signal posts, the decimal point before the last digit is not shown, and a reading of 132 would in fact mean 13.2.

Photographers inspired to record the journey on film, will be rewarded with many opportunities to capture the passing scenery. Since reflection from windows is a common problem, enthusiasts can compensate by keeping the camera lens close to the glass. Blur can be reduced by shooting at a 45-degree angle.

Each of the four routes in Enchanting Horizons is detailed from starting point to final destination, but the description of each route is easy to follow in either direction of travel.

Bon voyage!

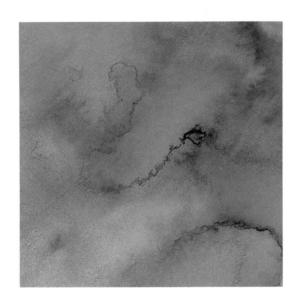

"…This passes not away!

This dew-drenched Range,

This infinite great width of open space,

This cool keen wind that blows like God's own breath…"

Arthur Stringer from "Morning in the North-West"

*C*ANADIAN

VIA Rail's premier train, the *Canadian*, is so close to the heart and history of this country that it's difficult to separate one from the other. It runs through the nation like an artery along 4,467 kilometres.

The pedigree of the *Canadian* reaches back to the creation of the first national railway line, constructed by the Canadian Pacific Railway in 1885. Comparing the size of the country's population at that time (a mere 4.5 million) to the scope of the project, there's no wonder it was called "an act of insane recklessness." Yet it was a huge success.

Seventy years later, gleaming stainless steel cars rolled onto the ribbon of steel from Toronto to Vancouver. The route has been modified since then, and today's *Canadian*, newly restored to its 1950s style, with modern amenities, takes the northern line through Winnipeg, Saskatoon, Edmonton, and Jasper.

The *Canadian* is the most prestigious of VIA's routes and travels through awe-inspiring landscapes, revealing the stark beauty of the Canadian Shield, the immense skies of

the Prairies and the grandeur of the Rocky Mountains through the panoramic windows of its stainless steel cars.

This description of the *Canadian's* route has been organized into sections according to the major stops on the Timetable. For reference, small maps for each section correspond to the text and the photographs.

ONTARIO

On this first leg of its epic journey across Canada, the *Canadian* rolls from the country's largest city through some of Canada's most sparsely populated regions. The panorama passing the train windows shifts from the glass towers of Toronto to the pine trees of Sioux Lookout, the transition covering 1,553 kilometres in slightly more than 24 hours.

Most of this part of the trip is in Ontario, the richest and most populous (with more than nine million people) Canadian province. This is where the nation's capital, Ottawa, and its largest city, Toronto, are located. The word Ontario means "shining waters" in the language of the Iroquois people, and it's an apt name, since the province contains one-fourth of the world's fresh water.

In Ontario there are not only the Great Lakes, but also countless small lakes.

Trains do not simply reveal the landscape, they create it. In Southern Ontario the connection between railroads and the development of Canada is apparent. The tracks are hemmed with office towers built by large financial companies have created a striking skyline, but the hundreds of thousands of new Canadians that have made Toronto their home have also given the city a vigourous, multicultural air.

The best way to see the layout of the

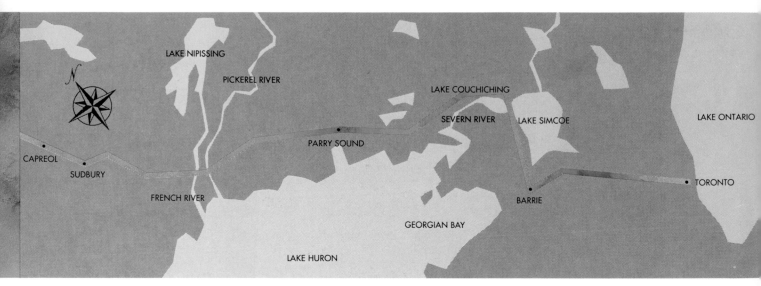

the factories and farms that both inspired and followed the laying of the rails. In the great northern wilderness, the few signs of civilization that exist usually are found near railroad tracks.

TORONTO

Toronto is Canada's commercial heart and Ontario's capital. Dramatic

land is with a visit to the CN Tower, at 180 stories, the world's tallest free-standing structure. From its observation gallery, Metropolitan Toronto (pop. 3.2 million) can be seen along the north shore of Lake Ontario, and on a clear day the view can stretch 100 kilometres. The lakeshore anchors several top attractions, including the exciting Harbourfront

Canadian National Archives

complex and the natural beauty of Toronto Islands Park.

It seems fitting that Toronto also has Canada's most impressive railway station. Union Station was built in 1927 as a cooperative effort between two great railways, the Canadian National and the

Canadian Pacific. The massive hall, with its arching coffered ceiling and pillars, is a fine example of the 1920s style of architecture. This multi-modal terminal provides access to an extensive railway network and is the heart of VIA's intercity services between Québec City, Montréal, Ottawa and Windsor. Also, it is well known to business commuters and

local travellers as well as those embarking on trips across the country.

Union Station is symbolic of the glorious adventure of a transcontinental train journey across Canada. The sounds of luggage wheels and the clicking heels of people rushing through the terminal resonate from the floors and walls, then become hushed in the high spaces between the arches. As passengers embark, they see the bright reflection of lights in the stainless steel of the *Canadian*, poised for its westward flight.

ALL ABOARD!

Mile 0 TORONTO

Centuries ago, the Huron tribes gave this area between the Humber and Don rivers the name Toronto, interpreted as "a place of meetings." It was a busy portage and trade route for indigenous peoples long before the French explorer Etienne Brulé put this area on the European map. Toronto was once a French trading post, then a British fort, before becoming the town of York. This fast-growing city later took back its original native Indian name. Leaving Toronto, the *Canadian* passes two unique structures – the slender CN Tower and the bulging SkyDome, the spectacular sports stadium with retractable roof.

Mile 63 BARRIE

Southern Ontario has some of the richest farmland in Canada, beautiful,

rolling countryside punctuated by neat woodlots. This region is called the Georgian Lakelands since it lies on the shores of Lake Huron's huge bay. Historically, it was called Huronia, after the native Indian nation that hunted and farmed here until the late 1600s.

Barrie (pop. 48,000) is on the shores of Kempenfelt Bay, an arm of Lake Simcoe, one of the largest bodies of water the *Canadian* will pass. The bay is famous for its coldness, depth, and lake trout. Barrie is a busy centre for water sports, especially scuba diving, and in winter the frozen bay attracts ice fishing enthusiasts and dog-sled teams.

From Barrie, the *Canadian* follows the shore to its sister city Orillia (pop. 25,000) at the north end of Lake Simcoe *(mile 86)*. Leaving Orillia, the train crosses the Severn River on a swing bridge and continues north along the shores of little Lake Couchiching, whose name means "water squeezed out."

Mile 150 PARRY SOUND

As soon as the *Canadian* crosses the Severn, it enters rock country, where hard stone ribs jut from the earth to mark the Canadian Shield, that region of billion-year-old rock that lies between the Great Lakes and Hudson Bay. Here, ancient glaciers scoured thousands of lakes, clean-bottomed and filled with remarkably clear water. On their rocky shores, outcroppings of granite, pink, gray and black, form rounded boulders, and in places the rock breathtakingly towers over the tracks.

On a deep harbour off Georgian Bay, Parry Sound (pop. 6,000) is a city of boats. Named after the Arctic explorer Sir William Parry, the town is the gateway to the world's largest concentration of islands, known as the 30,000 Islands.

Today the region is called Muskoka, the Lake Country, and is the recreational playground for the city dwellers of Southern Ontario. In autumn, the hardwoods, including Canada's signature maple, blaze gold and red.

Leaving Parry Sound, the *Canadian* crosses the Pickerel River *(mile 215)* and the French River *(mile 216)*, which was a vital link in the early days of the fur trade. Many names that have created Canada's history used this 112-kilometre stretch of shallow, swift-moving fresh water – Brulé in 1611, then Samuel de

Champlain, La Vérendrye, Mackenzie and Thompson. They were explorers whose names and deeds are remembered across the country.

Mile 262 SUDBURY

Approaching Sudbury (pop. 89,000), the landscape is a bizarre contrast between barren black slag heaps and white-barked birches. More than a million years ago, the Sudbury Basin, a unique depression 56 kilometres long and 27 kilometres wide, was created by volcanic action or the impact of a giant meteor. Scientists still debate the cause, but the result of the forces twisting the earth forced mineral-rich rock to the surface and blessed the area with an abundance of diverse resources.

The 381-metre INCO smokestack looms over the world's largest nickel mining and smelter complex, and an incredible 'lunar garden' that resulted from this development. Over the years, acid rain denuded the immediate landscape of vegetation, and mining waste created new hills. That damage is being countered by extensive environmental projects funded by the mining companies, including

reforestation projects that have created protected woodlands around the city.

Mile 276 CAPREOL

Around Capreol (pop. 3,800), the landscape becomes increasingly rugged and angular as the *Canadian* plunges into

"muskeg" a native Indian word describing unstable, wet and deep soil with high water content.

Capreol marks one of several *Railway Division Points,* following which the miles again begin to be measured from '0.'

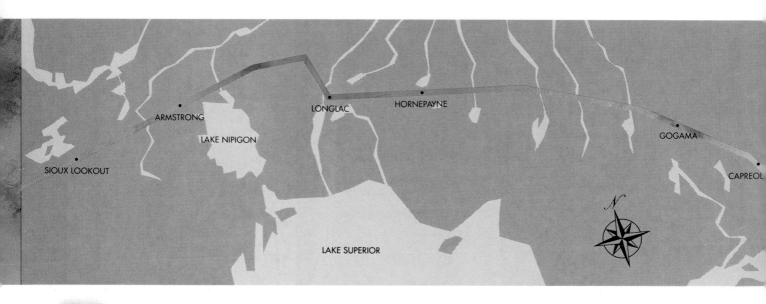

the thousand-mile gap of the Shield. The exposed bedrock is 500 million to five billion years old, creating a hard blanket for half of Canada and parts of the northern United States. Where it is thinly covered with soil, the land nurtures dense forests. But elsewhere, the landscape is a torturous combination of countless lakes and streams, and treacherous bogs called

Mile 86 GOGAMA

Gogama (pop. 700) is typical of the small, relatively isolated settlements along this section of the railway. They were created almost spontaneously in order to service locomotives, and were placed at approximately 240-kilometre intervals. But with the development of electric-diesel engines, many towns were erased from the map, to be remembered only in the names of sidings. The hamlets that remain support frontier economies based on logging, hunting and fishing. Bear and moose can be seen in this area.

Mile 296 HORNEPAYNE

Like most communities along this part of the *Canadian's* route, Hornepayne (pop. 1,800) started as a railway town, and the major industry today is the pulp mill. The railroads provided access to the immense forests, and lumber companies followed to develop the region.

The impact of the forest products industry is visible in the large clearcut areas, with piles of logs, and pulp and plywood plants that edge the tracks. Westbound from Caramat Lake, a large pole-producing mill is seen to the south.

Hornepayne is a *Railway Division Point*, following which the miles start again from '0.'

Mile 100 LONGLAC

Longlac (pop. 2,400) anchors the northern tip of Long Lake, 71 kilometres long and once an important part of the historic canoe route of the fur traders.

The multilingual town (52 percent of the population speak English and 44 percent speak French, four percent speak other languages) is committed to developing its outdoor leisure and recreation attractions.

One of the best descriptions of the elements, the rock, trees and water to be

seen in the Shield, was written by journalist William Hard in 1909. It still holds true: "It is a land where nature started to say something and stuttered a thousand times, an extraordinary region where there is one small landscape constantly shifting...."

Mile 243 ARMSTRONG

Entering Armstrong (pop. 1,500), look south for a view of Lake Nipigon, reaching 96 kilometres from north to south and measuring 64 kilometres at its widest point.

Armstrong is a *Railway Division Point* and a base for fly-in fishing and hunting camps in the region. The town

marks the change between Eastern and Central Time Zones *(watches should be adjusted either an hour back, if travelling westbound, or forward, if heading east).*

Mile 138 SIOUX LOOKOUT

This region of Ontario is called Sunset Country, where the lean black outlines of the spruce forest accentuate pink bands of falling light. Sioux Lookout (pop. 3,100) is the largest community since Sudbury. It's a centre for the pulp industry and is a *Railway Division Point*. Located on the English River-Lac Seul waterways, the town is a recreational centre for fishing and canoeing. Sioux Lookout hosts a blueberry festival in August. Between Sioux Lookout and Winnipeg, the *Canadian* is rarely interrupted by settlements.

▮Mile 12▮ HUDSON

Hudson (pop. 500) was once the air-freight centre of Canada, a testament to the pioneering bush pilots who developed early commercial air services in the uncharted north. Today, recreation has replaced exploration. With its lakes

▮Mile 137▮ MINAKI

The *Canadian* crosses the Winnipeg River, harbinger of the Prairies that are still beyond the horizon. Minaki (pop. 350) is a picturesque village on the river, just north of scenic Gun Lake. The historic Minaki Lodge, like the lodge in

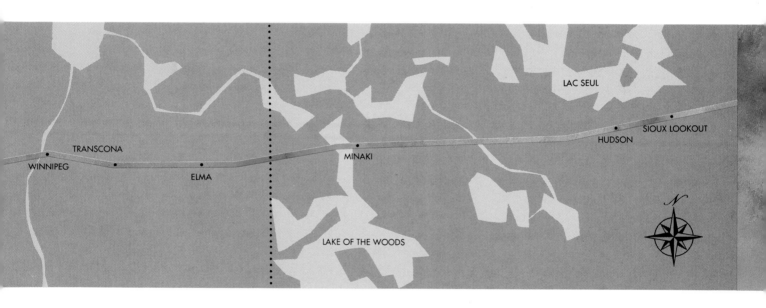

and forests, Hudson acts as the natural gateway to the Vermilion and Lac Seul waters, ideal for fishing, and hunting moose and bear. Hudson reached its zenith in 1926, the year of the gold rush in neighbouring Red Lake. In that year, more air freight passed through the Hudson airport than through any other in the country.

Alberta's Jasper National Park, was originally built to increase railway tourist traffic. This is Lake of the Woods country, famed for spectacular scenery and vivid sunsets. Leaving Minaki, the *Canadian* soon passes through the hamlet of Malachi *(mile 153)* with stunning views of its namesake lake. A waterfall cascades to the north.

Mile 159 ONTARIO-MANITOBA BORDER

A sign on the north side of the steel rails denotes the border. On the Manitoba side, the *Canadian* glides through the undeveloped forest and lakes of Whiteshell Provincial Park, on the western edge of the Shield. For Manitobans, the 1620-square-kilometre park is a Pre-Cambrian playground, especially known for canoeing and fishing. Its 200 lakes, some of them formed from meteor craters, offer some of the best northern pike, perch and lake trout fishing in Western Canada. Moose, caribou, eagles, beaver and deer live in the park, undisturbed by industry.

Mile 197 ELMA

From Elma (pop. 81), the *Canadian* runs arrow-straight due west to Winnipeg, only 88 kilometres away. The land opens into wide, level river valleys. The countryside becomes more pastoral, with farms that were originally given as land grants to entice settlers to the interior of Canada in the late 1800s.

Special "immigrant trains" were filled with pioneer settlers, and the Canadian National Railway created a

Canadian National Archives

service to help them find jobs and adjust to their new environment.

Mile 245 TRANSCONA

A 275-metre-long viaduct crosses the Red River Floodway, built after a 1950 flood forced the evacuation of

Winnipeg. From this eastern suburb, the downtown skyline of Winnipeg is straight ahead. The *Canadian* crosses 16 metres above the Seine River, and then the Red River, before arriving in Winnipeg. The city's rich history and diverse cultural blend are reflected in its people and its landmarks. It also offers world-class performing arts.

MANITOBA

Manitoba is one of the three Prairie provinces, the heartland of Canada, between the wilderness of Western Ontario and the foothills of the Rocky Mountains. The landscape was shaped by the glaciers of the Ice Age, which left a

Sometimes called the "keystone province" because of its location midway between the Atlantic and Pacific, Manitoba was originally so small it was known as the "postage stamp" province. Today it sprawls over 650,000 square kilometres, from the far north, where

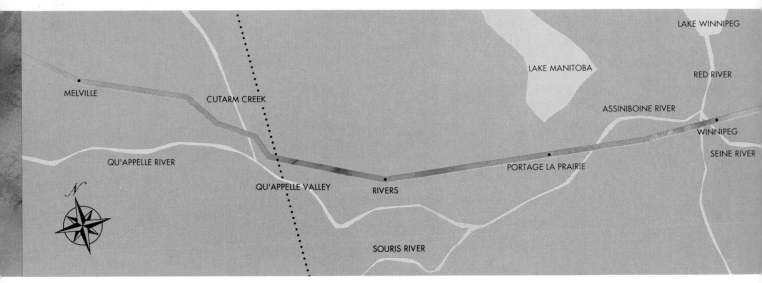

legacy of deep rivers and flat, rich tablelands. Prairie history began with the nomadic, bison-hunting native peoples, continued and then expanded with the arrival of the fur traders. The region was consolidated by the North West Mounted Police (later called the Royal Canadian Mounted Police) and transformed by the development of the railways.

Hudson Bay provides a saltwater port, to the south, where desert and cacti can be found. Entering Manitoba from the east, the *Canadian* passes the forests and lakes of the Pre-Cambrian Shield to the rolling prairie of the western lowlands, via the Lake Manitoba narrows. Land-locked Lake Manitoba is known for its freshwater fishing industry.

WINNIPEG

Winnipeg (pop. 600,000) is at the junction of three rivers that form a natural transportation hub. The silt-laden waters of the Red, the Assiniboine and the Seine inspired the Cree to call this place "Winni-nipi" – muddy water. These rivers are also responsible for establishing a diagonal street plan, unlike the grid system of most western cities, because early settlers marked property lines like spokes on a wheel radiating from the rivers. Today, the rivers cut the city into the distinctive neighbourhoods that give Winnipeg its character.

The city is a cosmopolitan centre, with a downtown area of modern towers mixed with heritage buildings, and older, established neighbourhoods where the homes are located along curved, tree-lined streets. The Exchange District's fine collection of turn-of-the-century commercial buildings inspired one of Winnipeg's nicknames, "the Chicago of the North." Selkirk Avenue expresses the multicultural heritage of the city, home to 50 ethnic groups. The Winnipeg Art Gallery owns the world's largest collection of Inuit sculpture and art. The suburb of St. Boniface is home to the largest French-speaking community outside Québec and many historic sites.

At the strategic fork of the rivers stands Union Station, built in 1911 to serve the many rail lines that made Winnipeg the crossroads of Canada. The station's massive dome, the interior of which is delicately plastered in pink and white, was designed by the same architects who created New York's famous Grand Central Station. The light-grey stone walls are faced with local Tyndall limestone, the final resting place of many prehistoric fossils, the seaweed, crabshells and ammonites from the ancient seabeds that once covered the Prairies.

ALL ABOARD!

Mile 0 WINNIPEG

The forks of the Red, Assiniboine and Seine rivers have been a meeting place for more than 8,000 years for the Cree and Assiniboine tribes, who made the vast Prairies their hunting preserve.

The region is also rich in European history, as the early explorers developed the fur trade and introduced their lifestyles from home.

Winnipeg is a modern industrial city. It is also the starting point for VIA's *Hudson Bay* train, which runs northward to Churchill, Manitoba's deep-sea port on Hudson Bay.

Leaving Winnipeg, the *Canadian* crosses the Assiniboine River, which flows into Lake Winnipeg, and passes the imposing Legislature Building. The 73-metre-high dome supports Manitoba's symbol, the Golden Boy, with a sheaf of wheat under his arm.

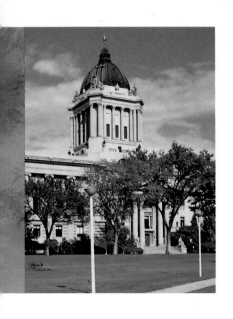

Mile 55 PORTAGE LA PRAIRIE

The name Portage La Prairie goes back to the time of the fur trade, when it was a resting area for voyageurs carrying their canoes between the Assiniboine River and Lake Manitoba. The French explorer and fur trader La Vérendrye built a key fort here in 1738. Portage La Prairie (pop. 21,000) is a major food processing centre in the middle of some of the richest farmland in the province.

Mile 143 RIVERS

Entering Rivers (pop. 2,000), the *Canadian* crosses the Minnedosa (Cree for "swift water") River on a 27-metre-long bridge *(mile 142)*. The town is a typical wheat-growing community, with grain elevators along the railway on one side and a business centre on the other.

Tall, brightly coloured grain elevators will be a common sight as the Prairies pass by. These sentinels of the plains have been called Canada's only indigenous architecture. The design is functional, making use of the way grain, like water, flows with gravity.

Mile 181 QU'APPELLE VALLEY

The spectacular scenery of the Qu'Appelle Valley spreads along the route of the *Canadian*, which follows the northern rim of the valley for about 50 kilometres. A series of shining lakes connected by the meandering Qu'Appelle River punctuates the valley floor like souvenirs from the Ice Age.

Several high bridges mark major rivers that flow north-south: Minnewashtack Creek's trestle *(mile 185)* is, at 467 metres, the longest bridge on the Prairies. En route will also be seen Birdtail Creek *(mile 191)*, Snake Creek *(mile 199)*, and the return to view of the mighty Assiniboine *(mile 205)*.

Mile 213 MANITOBA-
SASKATCHEWAN BORDER

After *mile 213*, watch for a sign that marks the boundary between Manitoba and Saskatchewan. The *Canadian* is near the mid-point of its transcontinental journey. The Prairie landscape of

world's largest known deposits of potash, lying in thick layers more than 1,000 metres beneath the wheatlands. The mineral, used in fertilizer production, is mined and taken to surface warehouses before being loaded into the rail tank cars waiting in the sidings.

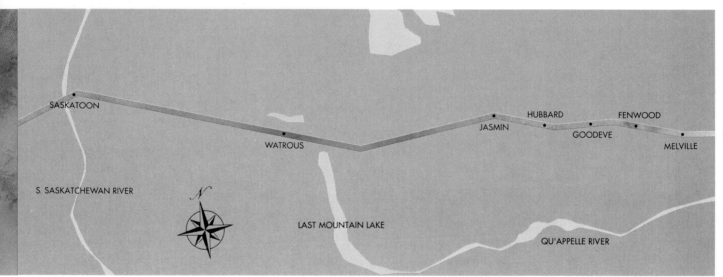

SASKATOON
WATROUS
JASMIN
HUBBARD
GOODEVE
FENWOOD
MELVILLE
S. SASKATCHEWAN RIVER
N
LAST MOUNTAIN LAKE
QU'APPELLE RIVER

undulating grain fields, which has been rolling by since Winnipeg, will become flatter as the train moves westward.

Mile 233 CUT ARM CREEK

From the 351-metre-long bridge over Cut Arm Creek, dome-shaped potash plants can be seen spreading over the Prairie. Saskatchewan holds the

Mile 280 MELVILLE

Melville (pop. 5,000) is the largest town on this section of the route, and is a *Railway Division Point*, from which the mileposts beside the track will start from '0' again. There's an interesting connection between this land-locked agricultural community and a world-famous maritime disaster. Melville was named for Charles Melville Hays, the president of the Grand Trunk Pacific Railroad Company that built this northern line. Hays died in the sinking of the Titanic in 1912.

The mix of cultures brought by the immigrants who flooded into the Prairies, following the railroads, can be seen in the churches that dominate the small towns. In Goodeve *(mile 18)*, two churches are particularly eye-catching, one single-steepled, and the other three-spired. Russian-Ukrainian settlers built the church in Hubbard, with its onion-shaped dome *(mile 28)*, and the one in Jasmin *(mile 42)*.

Mile 129 WATROUS

Watrous (pop. 2,000) is a resort community that exists because of the mineral hot springs of adjacent Little Manitou Lake. The lake has been famous for its curative qualities since before Europeans set foot on the Prairies; "manitou" means god or spirit in the Cree and Ojibway languages. The 19-kilometre-long lake has no outlet and no inflowing streams, and has accumulated salt for thousands of years, giving it greater buoyancy than the Dead Sea.

Mile 189 S. SASKATCHEWAN RIVER

A spectacular 457-metre-long bridge, one of seven over the South Saskatchewan River, brings the *Canadian* into Saskatoon, nicknamed the "City of Bridges."

Saskatoon began as a colony in the 1880s and is proud of its rich pioneer history and heritage.

SASKATCHEWAN

Saskatchewan, in the centre of the vast expanse of the Prairies, is known as the bread-basket of Canada. It produces 60 percent of the country's wheat and is home to some of the largest grain farms in the world. Though this fertile area is flat, there is variety elsewhere in the Saskatchewan landscape. The Cypress Hills in the southwest are, at 1,385 metres, the highest point in the province, and in the north lie the forests and lakes of the Canadian Shield.

The Plains tribes called this place "kisiskatchewan," meaning "swiftly flowing water," for the mighty river traversing their territory. The first Europeans used the Saskatchewan River as a major east-west route for their fur trade. As the region opened up, the North West Mounted Police force was formed, bringing law and order to the Prairies. A trickle of settlers became a flood after the railways were built, and the new province adopted the river's name.

Saskatchewan today is home to a million people, many with family roots in Russia, Scandinavia, Europe and the British Isles. Agriculture is the mainstay of the economy, but the province also has

a wealth of natural resources, including potash, uranium and oil.

SASKATOON

Saskatoon (pop. 185,000) sits in the midst of the Prairies like an oasis, a dark green band along the banks of the South berries – saskatoons – that grow in abundance along the river, and Lake thought them so delicious he took their name for the emerging town.

Saskatoon is the largest city in the province, and its economic hub. (The capital, Regina, is 160 kilometres to the

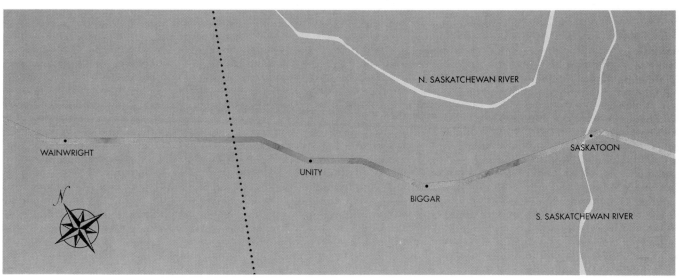

Saskatchewan River. The river bisects Saskatoon diagonally and is bridged in numerous places. The original settlement in 1882 was a temperance colony founded by John Lake and like-minded homesteaders who wished to escape the "evil influence of alcohol." Local legend has it that a native Indian brought Lake a handful of the purple misaskwatomin south.) Saskatoon is a leader in Canadian high-technology and mining industries. The city's prestigious University of Saskatchewan occupies 971 park-like hectares near the river.

This region is the historic heart of Saskatchewan, and the province's past is reflected in many nearby attractions. At Wanuskewin Heritage Park, just north of

Saskatoon, archaeological displays show the life of the indigenous peoples of 5,000 to 8,000 years ago. The Ukrainian Museum of Canada is a tribute to the early settlers of the province. To the north, Batoche National Historic Site was the battleground of the North West Rebellion in 1885, the last armed conflict on Canadian soil. Led by Louis Riel, the rebellion was the accumulation of years of frustration between the French-speaking Metis and the English-speaking population. The Metis, who were descendants of early white fur traders and Cree and Ojibway tribes, were valiantly trying to safeguard their language and cultural life. After a courageous struggle with the opposing militia, the Metis were defeated.

ALL ABOARD!

Mile 191 SASKATOON

Saskatoon developed slowly until the first railroad, a branch line from Regina, arrived in 1890. The site chosen for the station was on the opposite side of the river from the town, so most of the town was moved across the river. Then the Grand Trunk Pacific, the first northern transcontinental railway, arrived in 1906 and Saskatoon grew rapidly until it covered both sides of the South Saskatchewan River.

Mile 247 BIGGAR

This is a small (pop. 2,500) town with a sense of humour. Its slogan is "New York is big, but this is Biggar." It's in the prime grain-growing country of western Saskatchewan, and is a *Railway Division Point*, from which the distance mileage again starts at '0.'

Mile 57 UNITY

Unity (pop. 2,400) has a more diversified economy than most Prairie communities, due to local salt production plants. In 1946, oil exploration discovered a bed of rock salt 1,127 metres below the surface. It's mined by pumping water into mineshafts, and the resulting brine is pumped to the surface for purification into table salt.

Leaving Unity, the *Canadian* heads toward ranch country, and travellers can see the approach of rolling hills. Manitou Lake, to the north, is unusual for its size and for the island in its centre *(mile 90)*. Reflex Lake lies to the south *(mile 98)*.

Canadian National Archives

Mile 101 SASKATCHEWAN-
ALBERTA BORDER

This provincial boundary also
marks the division between Central and
Mountain Time Zones *(watches should be
set back an hour if westbound, or an hour
forward if eastbound).*

only 100 pairs remaining in the wild.

Oil and natural gas discoveries in
1921 made Wainwright the largest
community between Saskatoon and
Edmonton. Bobbing 'pumpjacks' mark
the hundreds of producing wells, almost
obscured by tall crops in summer, but

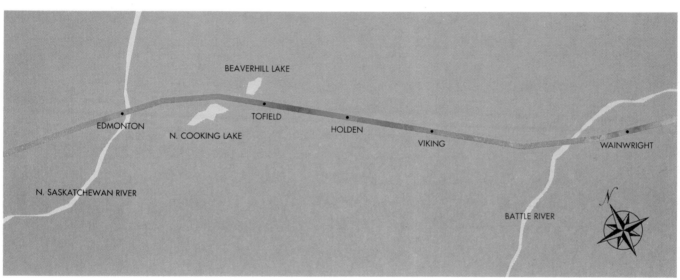

BEAVERHILL LAKE

EDMONTON

N. COOKING LAKE

TOFIELD

HOLDEN

VIKING

WAINWRIGHT

N. SASKATCHEWAN RIVER

BATTLE RIVER

N

Mile 140 WAINWRIGHT

Entering Wainwright (pop. 4,700),
the *Canadian* passes the restricted
grounds of Camp Wainwright, a
Canadian Forces training base. The
camp is also the site of the Canadian
Wildlife Service Peregrine Falcon
Hatchery. These fast, graceful birds are
an endangered species in Canada, with

starkly outlined against the black-and-
white fields of winter.

The *Canadian's* northern windows
reveal the panorama of the immense
Battle River Valley *(mile 147).* The train
makes an airy crossing 61 metres above
this impressive river on a steel trestle 884
metres long *(mile 149).* Numerous
sinkholes – places where the surface of

the ground has fallen, or been washed away – provide good habitat for migrating waterfowl, including the Canada goose. These ponds dot the landscape on both sides of the track.

Mile 184 VIKING

The town (pop. 1,160) is named in honour of the many Scandinavians who settled the area in the early 1900s.

The area was significant for the Plains tribes that hunted buffalo before the arrival of the Europeans. They left The Ribstones, two quartzite rocks painstakingly carved about 1,000 years ago, showing in relief a buffalo backbone and ribs. Pebbles and sand were used in making the carving; offerings were left at the rocks to ensure a successful hunt.

Mile 205 HOLDEN

The most striking sight in Holden (pop. 500) is the dramatic onion-shaped dome of the Holy Ghost Ukrainian Catholic Church. This east-central region of Alberta has many Eastern Byzantine-style churches, including Russian and Greek Orthodox, built by immigrant pioneers. The churches are usually simple frame structures like most Prairie buildings, but their individuality exists in their domes and spires. The interiors of the churches are often richly painted and decorated with icons.

Mile 226 TOFIELD

As the *Canadian* heads north, the landscape makes a transition to rugged bush and lakeland. The irregular hills are moraines deposited by the retreat of the glaciers more than 12,000 years ago. Huge Beaverhill Lake, an important stopover for many migrating bird species, can be seen to the north. Tofield (pop. 900) has an internationally renowned interpretive centre for bird-watching.

The tracks skirt the edge of the Cooking Lake-Blackfoot recreation, wildlife and grazing area. Adjacent is Elk Lake National Park. Moose, elk, coyote and ruffed grouse are commonly sighted in the region. To the south *(mile 240)* lies North Cooking Lake.

Mile 260 N. SASKATCHEWAN RIVER

The 504-metre-long Clover Bar Bridge carries the *Canadian* into Edmonton across the North Saskatchewan River. The fringe of oil refineries on the outskirts of the city are reminders of Alberta's huge wealth of petroleum resources. The city's dramatic skyline features the majestic dome of the Alberta Legislature Building.

ALBERTA

Alberta has a variety of scenery. In addition to the rolling grasslands in the south, the lakes and forests of the north, and the parkland between those regions, Alberta has the rugged foothills and eastern slopes of the great Rocky

Unlike the provinces the *Canadian* has already crossed, Alberta did not take its name from a native Indian language. It was named for Queen Victoria's fourth daughter, Princess Caroline Alberta, when the territory became a province in 1905. But, like the other Prairie

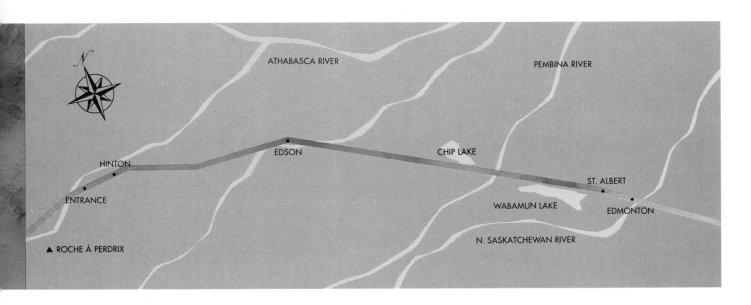

Mountains. The difference in terrain is reflected in the province's economy. There are more beef cattle ranches than anywhere else in Canada, most of them in the foothills, where the steep slopes and dry land are not suitable for crops. The provincial flower is the wild rose.

provinces, Alberta has a history that includes a colourful mix of native peoples and multicultural immigrants, railroaders and voyageurs, explorers and farmers. Today, most of Alberta's 2.5 million people live in the two largest cities, Calgary and Edmonton.

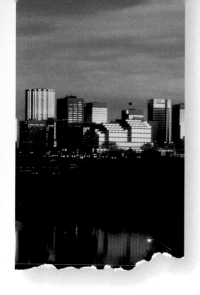

EDMONTON

Edmonton (pop. 850,000) was incorporated in 1904, but it's been a Canadian boomtown from its fur trading days and the time of the Yukon gold rush, right through the huge Alberta oil discoveries of 1947. Economic well-being and an enthusiastic lifestyle are the trademarks of the city. The amazing, enormous West Edmonton Mall rates seven mentions in the Guinness Book of World Records.

Edmonton sprawls on both sides of the twisting North Saskatchewan River, covering more territory than any other Canadian city (681 square kilometres). The riverbanks are the pride of the city, and form a 27-kilometre greenbelt that has made Edmonton famous for its parks. The city is also known for special events and has adopted the name "Canada's Festival City."

ALL ABOARD!

Mile 0 EDMONTON

Edmonton can trace its beginnings to a pair of rival fur trading forts, Augustus and Edmonton House, built and rebuilt in several locations along the North Saskatchewan River between 1795 and 1873. These two fur trading companies opened up the area which drew explorers westward. Later, the Yukon gold rush in 1897 brought thousands of 'Klondikers' through

Edmonton and made the community the gateway to the north. The arrival of the transcontinental railway in 1905 established Edmonton as a crossroad, but the seal of the city's success was oil. Travelling through Edmonton, the *Canadian* passes gleaming skyscrapers, green parks, and huge refineries.

Mile 6 ST. ALBERT

Leaving Edmonton, the *Canadian* passes the satellite community of St. Albert, seven kilometres northwest on the Sturgeon River. This community was founded as a mission in 1861 by a farsighted priest, Father Albert Lacombe. He realized that the herds of bison that the Metis depended on for their livelihood would soon be extinct, and established a settlement with large gardens and grain fields. St. Albert Mission was the site of the first school, orphanage and hospital in what is now Alberta. Father Lacombe died in 1916.

Mile 44 WABAMUN LAKE

The *Canadian* bridges an arm of Wabamun Lake, which is so calm it was named after the Cree word for "mirror." In summer, it's a popular spot for canoeists and fishermen seeking northern pike, yellow perch and whitefish; in winter, the smooth ice attracts skaters.

This area has been a major coal producer for almost 100 years, and two above-ground mines can be visited. Several coal-fired power-generating stations are on the shores, including the Sundance Power Plant, the largest in the province.

Mile 67 PEMBINA RIVER

The first major river-crossing on this leg of the *Canadian's* route is the 274-metre-long bridge over the Pembina, a narrow rushing river that was used as a route to British Columbia's Cariboo gold fields in the 1860s.

Over the next 70 kilometres, the train will bridge five rivers, including the Lobstick River, twice *(miles 72 and 100)* and Carrot Creek *(mile 105)*. The highest spans on this section are the 40-metre bridges over Wolf Creek *(mile 122.1)* and the McLeod River *(mile 122.6)*.

The Lobstick takes its name from a signal device used by the early fur traders and railway surveyors who first mapped these deeply forested hills and mountains. Needing to devise a communication system of sorts, they would select a tall tree that stood out from the rest, and cut off, or lob, all the lower branches. This beacon tree – called a lobstick – was used to mark meeting places and safe river crossings.

Canadian National Archives

Mile 129 EDSON

Rolling, green forest surrounds the community of Edson (pop. 4,000), midway between Edmonton and Jasper National Park, the gateway to the Rocky Mountains. The first view of the Rockies from the *Canadian* is the Miette Range to the south *(mile 139)*.

Mile 184 HINTON

The *Canadian* continues to climb steadily through the encroaching foothills that preview the majestic peaks ahead. The tracks rise to an impressive elevation of 1,058 metres *(mile 177)*.

Hinton (pop. 9,000) is rapidly growing into a city. At the turn of the century, it served the coal fields that extended east to Edson and southwest into what is now Jasper National Park. Today, Hinton is a centre for winter sports and is well-known for Nordic skiing. To the north is William A. Switzer Provincial Park, noted for excellent canoeing on five interconnected lakes.

Mile 189 ENTRANCE

A 'sea of mountains' lies before the *Canadian* at the official start to the Rockies. The train crosses the Athabasca River *(mile 193)*, which originates in the Columbia Icefields within Jasper National Park. The river is Canada's

seventh-longest, flowing 1,231 kilometres into Lake Athabasca.

Many famous names in the exploration of Canada travelled the Athabasca, including Alexander Mackenzie and David Thompson. They worked for rival fur trading companies, and in searching for new trapping country added many 'discoveries' to European

maps. Another important explorer, Etienne Brulé, gave his name to the lake *(mile 197-205)*. The *Canadian* skirts the slopes of Lac Brulé on its way to the boundary of Jasper National Park.

JASPER NATIONAL PARK

Jasper National Park is one of the country's most-photographed places. It's been called "the gem of the Rockies," and remains unspoiled despite the more than two million people who visit every year. Jasper National Park, measuring 10,878 square kilometres, is the largest of Canada's four Rocky Mountain Parks, which were collectively declared a World Heritage Site by UNESCO in 1984.

The Rockies are not just one line of mountains, but the edge of the Western Cordillera, a complex jumble of plateaus, folded rock layers and recent (in geologic terms) volcanoes that stretches to the Pacific Coast.

Waterfalls, gorges and jagged peaks echo one another's beauty throughout the park. There's Sunwapta Falls, whose name is a Stoney Indian word for "turbulent river," Maligne Canyon, and the awesome Columbia Icefield, 389 square kilometres of glaciers, deep

SNARING RIVER

SNAKE INDIAN RIVER

▲ PYRAMID MOUNTAIN

▲ ▲ VICTORIA CROSS RANGE

DEVONA SIDING

BRULÉ LAKE

MIETTE RIVER

PARK GATE

ATHABASCA RIVER

JASPER

▲ ROCHE MIETTE

ENTRANCE

▲ ROCHE À PERDRIX

▲

▲ ▲ ▲ MIETTE RANGE

THE WHISTLERS

ROCKY RIVER

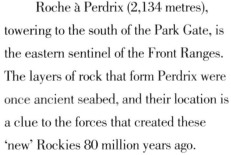

crevasses and jagged rock peaks. Even more important than its beauty is Jasper National Park's role as a wildlife sanctuary. Bighorn sheep and mountain goats patrol the peaks, black bear and moose wade the streams, and grizzly bears go berrying on the Alpine meadows.

Mile 206 PARK GATE

The *Canadian* enters Jasper National Park via the Athabasca River Valley, and follows the river into the heart of the park. The valley forms a natural division across the park, between the easternmost Front Ranges of the Rockies, and the Main Ranges west of Jasper townsite.

Roche à Perdrix (2,134 metres), towering to the south of the Park Gate, is the eastern sentinel of the Front Ranges. The layers of rock that form Perdrix were once ancient seabed, and their location is a clue to the forces that created these 'new' Rockies 80 million years ago.

Across the valley to the south, Roche Miette (2,316 metres) is notable for its sheer limestone cliff rising 300 metres at the end of the Miette Range. Behind the range are the Miette

Hotsprings, the hottest mineral pools in the Canadian Rockies.

Disaster Point *(mile 204)* is a stark mass of rock that drops almost straight down to the Athabasca River, except where it was blasted for the railbed. The Point's salty mineral licks make it a popular hangout for bighorn sheep and mountain goats.

Mile 215 DEVONA SIDING

This was the site of the original Jasper House, a fur trade supply post built in 1813 by Jasper Hawes, a merchant who became so well-known his name settled over the whole area.

The Rocky River flows into the Athabasca from the south, and the Snake Indian River from the north, creating the shallow backwater of Jasper Lake. Though Jasper Lake is large, it is not constant, filling up in summer and emptying to nothing in winter.

Mile 225 HENRY HOUSE

Crossing the Snarling River, the *Canadian* continues toward Jasper townsite. The valley below was once the site of the first supply post in the area, built by fur traders in 1811. This part of the Athabasca River Valley is known as the Elk Range. Jasper National Park has a healthy population of more than 2,000 elk, and one of the larger herds grazes in these dry, open meadows. Because elk and other animals need grasslands for food, park wardens occasionally light

Mile 235 JASPER

The townsite of Jasper and its focal point, Jasper Station, lie at the northern end of Jasper National Park, where the Athabasca and Miette rivers meet. The distinctive architecture of Jasper Station gives it an English manor air, and uses

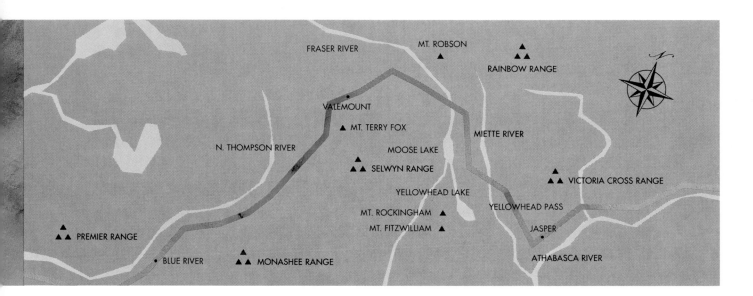

controlled forest fires (called prescribed burns) to keep the forest cover low.

Across the Athabasca River is beautiful green Lac Beauvert. The unusual colours of the lakes throughout the park come from glacial silts in the waters. The far side of the lake is the site of world-famous Jasper Park Lodge, a unique hotel with a loyal following.

decorative stonework of local fieldstones. Approximately 4,000 residents live in harmony with local wildlife. It is not unusual to see elk and mule deer casually stroll down Main Street.

The delightful town has attractive shops, a variety of eateries and numerous nightspots. It is the hub from where visitors can join in numerous activities throughout the year. In winter, there are excellent cross-country track-set trails radiating throughout the park. During the summer, visitors have the chance to walk the trail which leads from the Icefields Parkway to the famed Athabasca Glacier.

ALL ABOARD!

Mile 0 JASPER

Jasper is also the starting point for VIA's westbound *Skeena* train, which follows the same tracks as the *Canadian* through the Yellowhead Pass before diverging northwest to the port city of Prince Rupert.

Leaving Jasper, the *Canadian* glides past The Whistlers (2,470 metres), easily identified by the aerial tramway lodge that crowns the top.

Mile 6 VICTORIA CROSS RANGE

The tracks climb imperceptibly along the Miette River to Yellowhead Pass, hugging the rugged rock face of the Victoria Cross Range. These mountains of the Rockies' Main Ranges are distinctively darker than the 'new' Front Ranges, and older, being formed from rust-coloured quartz sandstone 175 million years ago.

The wire fences that sometimes appear on the uphill side of the track are slide detectors, which activate a warning signal for train engineers in case of a rockslide or avalanche.

The wide valley bottom is boggy Dominion Prairie *(mile 10)*. It is a favourite spot for moose and elk, coyotes and hawks.

Mile 17 YELLOWHEAD PASS

The crest of the Yellowhead Pass is the border between Alberta and British Columbia and the division between Mountain and Pacific Time Zones.

(Watches should be set back an hour if westbound, or forward if eastbound.) The pass was put on the European map by David Thompson, who was informed of its location by the local native people. Various tribes had used the pass as a trading route for centuries, and the fur traders followed suit to such an extent they called it Leather Pass, for all the skins shipped over it.

It is one of the lowest points in the entire North American Continental Divide. The track elevation is 1,131 metres, but many surrounding peaks are more than 3,000 metres. From the Continental Divide, all water systems flow either east or west.

Mile 22 YELLOWHEAD LAKE

The *Canadian* skirts the shore of narrow Yellowhead Lake, with its spectacular backdrop of Mount Fitzwilliam and Mount Rockingham. A lake, a mountain pass, a highway and a town all bear the name Yellowhead. *(A brief explanation of this historic name may be read on page 57.)* This magnificent rangeland was once home to the Interior Salish and Athabaskan peoples.

Mile 36 MOOSE LAKE

Narrow Moose Lake, six kilometres long, presents one of the best photo opportunities on this section. The Selwyn Range is striking, its steep forested slopes etched with rocky gullies and a waterfall *(mile 36)*.

At the west end of the lake *(mile 44)*, the clear waters of the Fraser River appear almost level with the tracks. The *Canadian* enters a 500-metre tunnel that was built to reduce the danger of avalanches *(mile 48)*. At Glacier Creek a waterfall can be glimpsed to the south *(mile 50)*.

Mile 52 MOUNT ROBSON

Often referred to as the "Monarch of the Canadian Rockies," Mount Robson is also known as "The Dome," accurately describing the grandeur of the sheer rock sides graced with a tiara of snow. Mount Robson Provincial Park was created in 1913 to preserve the peak and surrounding area.

The *Canadian* will be in sight of Mount Robson for 16 kilometres before turning sharply south *(mile 65)* and continuing to descend. To the east, Mount Terry Fox (2,676 metres) is a memorial to

the young Canadian who, after losing a leg to cancer, ran across the country in 1980 to promote cancer research. After his death, a monument was erected in his honour in Vancouver.

Mile 74 VALEMOUNT

Valemount (pop. 700) is located in the Rocky Mountain Trench, that brief interruption between the Rockies and three mountain ranges to the west: the Cariboo, Monashee, and Selkirk. Valemount is a lumber town on a long arm of water that was created by the huge Mica Dam almost 100 kilometres to the south.

The *Canadian* climbs from Valemount, then levels off for the fastest portion of track on this section. The flat land on either side of the tracks is muskeg, unstable swamp that swallowed beds of logs before the tracks could be laid on top.

The Albreda Glacier is visible as a high band of white, gleaming on top of the mountains to the west *(mile 92)*. Pyramid Falls is briefly visible close to the tracks on the east side, like a partly collapsed set of rock shelves *(mile 113)*. The North Thompson River appears from the west and follows the tracks into Blue River *(mile 106)*.

Mile 132 BLUE RIVER

Blue River (pop. 600), home to one of the province's heli-skiing outfitters, is

a popular recreation centre for fishing, and has an excellent trail system with easy access for the disabled.

The town marks a *Railway Division Point* and the mileposts will again begin to be numbered from '0.'

The wide valley with its muskeg

Mile 67 CLEARWATER

For the previous 56 kilometres, the *Canadian* has been criss-crossing the North Thompson, as the railway surveyors did almost 100 years ago, seeking the best places to lay tracks. The mountains are low and rounded, with

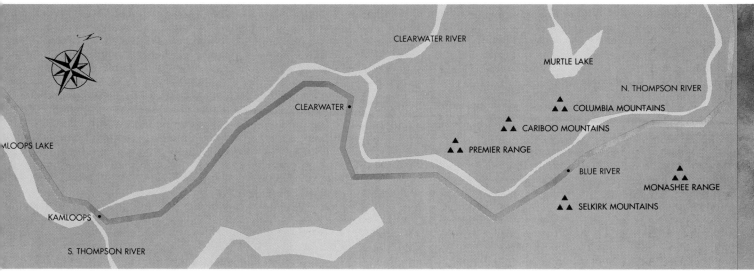

bottom begins to close in upon the tracks, and the *Canadian* will wind through a narrow gorge called Porte D'Enfer (Gate of Hell) *(mile 8-18)*. One short tunnel is a perfect rock arch *(mile 12)*.

Eastward, the river makes an 'S' turn; the roiling green waters racing through the channel below are called Little Hell's Gate *(mile 16)*.

clearcut patches on their flanks. This region is dotted with small lumber mills, marked by the rounded cones of their furnaces and the surrounding stacks of logs and lumber.

At Clearwater (pop. 400), the Clearwater River joins the North Thompson. This lumber and farming community is the entrance to Wells Gray

Canadian National Archives

Provincial Park and Recreation Area, one of British Columbia's exceptional wilderness reserves. Downstream, at Little Fort, is one of the province's few remaining reaction ferries, which takes cars across the river with only the current for propulsion *(mile 91)*.

Mile 139 KAMLOOPS

The North Thompson meets its sister river, the South Thompson, and flows into Kamloops Lake. The city was originally a settlement of overlanders, who trekked across the Rockies in search of gold.

PROFILE

Kamloops (pop. 67,000) is the main city of British Columbia's high country. The dry interior of the province encompasses the rolling hills of ranch country, deep river canyons and many high-altitude lakes.

Kamloops lies at the junction of the North and South Thompson Rivers, and at the east end of long, narrow Kamloops Lake. The signature of Kamloops is the aromatic dust from sagebrush-covered hills. Kamloops is a centre for outdoor activities and is one of the finest fishing

areas in the province. Ranching is the predominant industry.

BRITISH COLUMBIA

This westernmost Canadian province (pop. 3.2 million) is known for its spectacular scenery and for Vancouver, one of the world's loveliest cities. Though the province contains a variety of geophysical and climatic regions, the basic elements of British Columbia's beauty are mountains and water.

The Rocky Mountains run the length of the province from the southeast to the northwest, flanked by a series of companion ranges – Columbia, Monashee, Cariboo, Selkirk, Purcell, Cassiar, Omineca and Skeena. These mountains are the sources of six major rivers: the Fraser, Columbia, Peace, Skeena, Yukon and Liard.

British Columbia is where the Canadian landmass meets the Pacific Ocean. The coastline stretches more than 17,000 kilometres in a convoluted pattern of islands and fjords. The wealth of natural resources and inspiring scenery has created an economy based on forestry, mining, tourism and agriculture.

ALL ABOARD!

Mile 0 KAMLOOPS

The name Kamloops comes from the Salish people, who called it "meeting of the waters." The original Fort Kamloops was built as a trading post in

tracks hug the north shore of Kamloops Lake beneath the bluffs as they pass through three tunnels. The first of many crossings of the Thompson River is on a bridge 18 metres above the water, giving passengers dramatic views of a narrowing canyon *(mile 28)*.

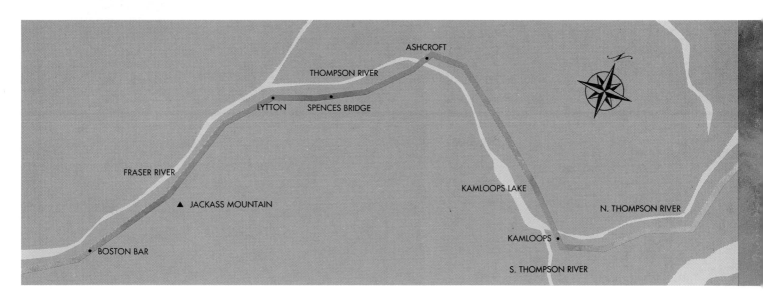

1812. The area boomed during the 1862 Cariboo Gold Rush, and by the time railway construction crews came through in 1885, Kamloops was an established town. Today, some of the biggest cattle ranches in the world can be found just outside Kamloops.

Westbound, the *Canadian* bridges the North Thompson for the last time. The

Mile 48 ASHCROFT

Ashcroft (pop. 1,900) gets only 18 centimetres of precipitation a year, earning it the title of "the driest town in Canada." The landscape is desert-like, and both cactus and sage grow in abundance. Erosion has created odd formations from the reddish bluffs, such as hoodoos, isolated pinnacles of rock

that remain after a hill has worn away.

The *Canadian* continues through the Thompson's Black Canyon *(mile 51-53)*, high above the turbulent white water. Most of the way into Vancouver, the tracks will wind from canyon to canyon along a trench called "avalanche alley."

Mile 75 SPENCES BRIDGE

Crossing the river at this point was an important stage on the route to the Cariboo Gold Rush. In 1864, an enterprising Mr. Spence built the first bridge and charged a toll for users. Just beyond the bridge on the west side of the river is Murray Creek Falls, which shoots out from the mountainside in the spring.

The dramatic Rainbow Canyon *(mile 80-95)* is a scenic dream and a railway construction nightmare. The numerous tunnels, slidesheds and bridges coaxed from almost vertical walls are a triumph of engineering. The names along this stretch paint pictures of the menacing terrain: Jaws of Death Gorge *(mile 85-90)*, Suicide Rapids *(mile 87)*, and Cape Horn *(mile 93)*.

Mile 95 LYTTON

The tiny town of Lytton (pop. 370) is at the junction of the Thompson and Fraser Rivers. For a distance, the distinct waters of the two rivers flow side by side in the same channel. The Fraser has changed dramatically since it crossed the *Canadian's* route near the Yellowhead Pass, and flows dark brown with silt from mountain runoff. The Thompson is clear after being filtered through a lake system. Lytton is a centre for rafting and canoe trips on both rivers.

The *Canadian* heads almost due south toward Hope and the exit of the Fraser River Canyon. En route, the train passes over the Cisco bridges *(mile 103)*, 247 metres long and 67 metres above the torturous rapids, said to be among the

most spectacular crossings in North America. Jackass Mountain, named for the pack animals of the gold rush trail, was called the "hill of despair," but the *Canadian* avoids angst by tunnelling through *(mile 109)*.

Mile 125 BOSTON BAR

At Boston Bar (pop. 500) the bed of the Fraser is full of jagged boulders, and the pent-up force of the water is ready to reach a crescendo. Hell's Gate *(mile 7)* is the most famous stretch of rapids in British Columbia, a by-product of the blasting needed to lay the rail and roadbeds. The Fraser is so strong in this narrow channel that a fish ladder was built to help salmon swim upstream to spawn. An aerial tramway descends 152 metres to water level for a close look at the courageous canoeists and weary salmon venturing through the white waters.

The mouth of the Fraser River Canyon is punctuated by Lady Franklin Rock *(mile 27)*, a massive black boulder. It is named for the wife of English explorer Sir John Franklin. She came in search of her husband after his disappearance in 1845. She was unable to go farther, and his remains were eventually found in the Arctic.

Mile 40 HOPE

At Hope (pop. 4,000), the mountains suddenly fall back and form a distant ring around the lush Fraser Valley. This rich farmland is the Delta, formed by the silt deposited by the Fraser River after its rush through the province. The flat green fields are a reflective pastoral interlude between the stone canyons of the mountains and the steel and glass canyons of downtown Vancouver.

The river is broad and slow, divided by islands and travelled by boats. Sixty kilometres to the south, in Washington State, the snow-brushed peak of Mount Baker (3,285 metres) seems to float above the horizon. Nearer, the sharp peaks of the Coast Mountains form a backdrop for

Through the years, the local Chehalis tribe has recounted many stories of the elusive legendary Sasquatch, a creature so powerful that the hairy giant can wrestle bears. Belief in the mythical creature's existence has grown far and wide.

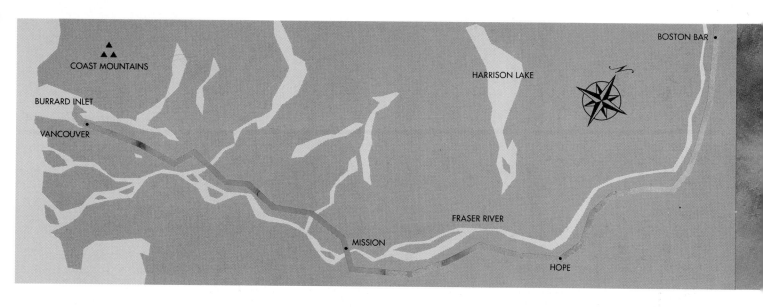

Canada's third-largest city. Across the Fraser River, Agassiz *(mile 58)* boasts the oldest wooden railroad station still in existence in British Columbia. Originally built in 1893, it was restored in 1985 and renovated into a local museum and archives. It was the station stop for Harrison Hot Springs, a popular lakeside resort and spa, with mineral pools.

Mile 87 MISSION

The *Canadian* crosses the Fraser for the last time at Mission. The area was first settled by Roman Catholic missionaries, who established a mission in 1861. Westminster Abbey, one of two Benedictine monasteries in Canada, was established almost a hundred years later; its beautiful church is just east of town.

Mile 131 VANCOUVER

Passing through the outskirts of Vancouver, the train rides along a deep cut that conceals from view the surrounding neighbourhoods, as the final kilometres of track lead into the downtown railyards.

The Pacific Central Station, a multi-modal facility, is an imposing stone structure that was built in 1919 and is fronted by Thornton Park, a relaxing oasis of greenery. The station is on the eastern edge of downtown, facing the waters of False Creek, site of Expo '86. An added boon to travellers, Vancouver's speedy SkyTrain system makes a stop just across the street.

PROFILE

Vancouver's character is its fantastic setting between the Pacific Coast and the dark green forests of the Coast Mountains. Having set out from Britain, Captain George Vancouver discovered the entrance to Puget Sound. In 1792, he founded the city that would later bear his name. It quickly gained notoriety as an important seaport, and a century later, the colony achieved independence from Britain. Though the

William Surgenor Collection

In 1904, Mission was the starting point for the first train robbery in Canadian history, carried out by the well-known outlaw Bill Miner. After boarding the westbound train, Miner and two accomplices stopped it at Silverdale *(mile 92)* and got away with $7,000.

ocean played a major role in Vancouver's growth, the city remained isolated from the rest of Canada. Then in 1885, the transcontinental railroad arrived, uniting the country and also establishing Vancouver as the dominant city of Canada's Pacific coast. Vancouver was incorporated in 1886, and grew from 1,000 residents to 20,000 by the year 1896.

The city is poised on the rim of the Pacific, and is a commercial and communications centre for Western Canada. The landmark buildings of Vancouver's dynamic skyline give clues to the city's economic and cultural life. Under the white sails that form the roof of the Canada Place complex are trade, convention and cruise centres. The domed B.C. Place stadium is used for sports, entertainment and expositions, and the easily recognized green roof of the Hotel Vancouver marks the centre of the city's downtown shopping area and financial district.

Vancouver (pop. 1.5 million) is home to half the people in British Columbia, an ethnic mix reflected in the neighbourhoods that characterize the city. Its Chinatown is the second-largest in

North America, and Granville Island is a friendly marketplace for foods, arts and crafts on the shore of False Creek. In the spring, cherry blossoms can be seen along many streets, and parks are everywhere. The most important of these and very dear to the hearts of

Vancouverites is Stanley Park, on the edge of the downtown centre.

The Strait of Georgia separates Vancouver from Vancouver Island, whose mountains are backlit by the setting sun. The Island is home to Victoria, the capital city of British Columbia and the starting point for VIA's *Malahat* train.

"At the Battle of the Leaves the transparent salmon

Comes up the stream to seek the shaman's spear

The shaman's body turns four times in the whirlpool

It is his own soul threshing on the spear."

Floris McLaren from "North West Coast"

S KEENA

VIA Rail's *Skeena* train connects with the *Canadian* at Jasper, and shares the same track westward over the Yellowhead Pass. Its 1,160-kilometre route takes you down the slope of the Rocky Mountains, across the Interior Plateau of British Columbia and through the Bulkley Valley, en route to the Skeena River Valley, which it will follow all the way to Prince Rupert on the Pacific Coast.

On the last 300 kilometres of its trip, the train follows the north bank of the mighty Skeena (a Gitksan Indian word meaning "river of mists"). The river's sheer canyons, high trestles and foaming green rapids are beautiful, but often mist-shrouded.

British Columbia's history is close to the surface along the *Skeena's* route. The ancient traditions of the native peoples, the not-too-distant pioneer days of gold-panning and sternwheelers, and modern history, have all left their marks at the side of the tracks.

ALL ABOARD!

Mile 0 JASPER

From the town of Jasper in the wide bottom of the Athabasca River Valley, the *Skeena* climbs the Main Ranges of the Rocky Mountains to Yellowhead Pass (elevation 1,058 metres), one of the lowest points in the North American Continental Divide.

The western slopes of the Rockies receive plenty of rain. The resulting wet belt supports giant cedars and hemlock, species which will not be seen again until the *Skeena* nears the Pacific Ocean.

(For more information on Jasper and the start of the Skeena's route, please refer to the description of the Canadian's route that appears on pages 38 to 39.)

Mile 43 REDPASS JUNCTION

At Redpass Junction, the routes of the *Canadian* and the *Skeena* part, with the *Canadian* heading south to Kamloops and Vancouver, and the *Skeena* rolling northwest to Prince Rupert. Redpass is a *Railway Division Point*, where the

Mile 17 REARGUARD FALLS

The Fraser River is a beautiful blue channel winding north of the tracks. To the south, Rearguard Falls is the final barrier to spawning salmon in their 1,200-kilometre migration from the sea. During August and September, Chinook

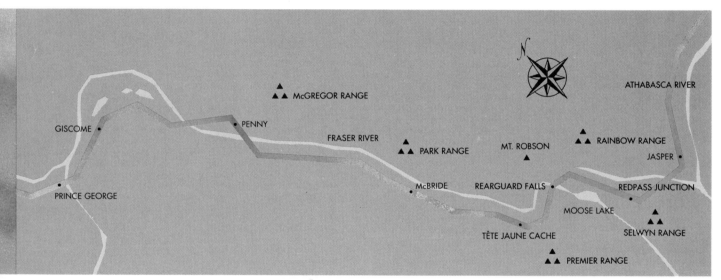

GISCOME •

PENNY •

McGREGOR RANGE ▲ ▲

FRASER RIVER

PARK RANGE ▲ ▲

MT. ROBSON ▲

RAINBOW RANGE ▲ ▲

ATHABASCA RIVER

JASPER •

• PRINCE GEORGE

McBRIDE •

REARGUARD FALLS •

REDPASS JUNCTION •

MOOSE LAKE

SELWYN RANGE ▲ ▲

TÊTE JAUNE CACHE •

PREMIER RANGE ▲ ▲

mileposts begin to be numbered from '0.'

The view is dominated by Mount Robson (3,953 metres), the highest peak in the Canadian Rockies, standing bare-rock head-and-shoulders above its neighbours. Nicknamed "The Dome," Robson is often wreathed in cloud, but is always impressive, and on a clear day its sheer rock faces are awesome.

salmon, characterized by bold round spots on the back and the entire tail, can be seen attempting to leap the 10-metre falls. A few heavier than 31 kilograms are taken every year.

Taverna *(mile 20)* is another *Railway Division Point*, where the numbering of the mileposts will again begin at '0.'

Canadian National Archives

Mile 4 TÊTE JAUNE CACHE

This tiny community (pop. 41) takes its name from a 19th-century Iroquois trapper and guide for the Hudson's Bay Company, Pierre Hatsinaton, who is also remembered in the names of Yellowhead Pass and Lake. (Of part-European ancestry, Hatsinaton had light-coloured hair, and was nicknamed Yellow Head – or Tête Jaune, to the French voyageurs.) He was said to have stored a fortune in furs between Tête Jaune Cache and Yellowhead Pass, but it was never found.

The town was important during the late 1800s as the head of navigation for the stern-wheelers on the Fraser River. In the early 1900s, Tête Jaune Cache was a major railway construction town. Now, local businesses provide outfitting for heli-skiing, kayaking and guest ranches.

Mile 43 McBRIDE

McBride (pop. 550) is in the Robson Valley on the fertile benchlands of the Fraser River, and is surrounded by the Rocky and Cariboo Mountains. It is named for British Columbia's youngest premier (Richard McBride, premier from 1903-15), in whose day it was a railway boomtown known as Siding 39. Most of the population of 2,500 left when the track construction crews moved on, but the original Grand Trunk Pacific Railway station is a reminder of the town's heyday.

Moose are plentiful from here to Prince George. Old forest fires created large areas of the open bush that is prime moose habitat. The animals are especially visible along the sides of the river on summer evenings and in winter.

Mile 69 PENNY

Between McBride and Prince George is one of the loneliest stretches of the *Skeena's* route. Several small communities, such as Penny (pop. 32), are the only settlements. The tracks twist along the Fraser River, hemmed by farmland. The background forests gradually change from wet-belt cedar and hemlock to a sub-Alpine mix of deciduous and coniferous trees, and fields of wildflowers.

The Fraser makes a loop to the north while the *Skeena* crosses over its tributary, the Bowron River *(mile 101)*. The Bowron is full of spawning salmon in summer, a movable feast for the grizzly bears that range the upper reaches of the river. From March to October, moose, beaver and osprey frequent the area, which includes a world-famous canoe circuit in Bowron Lake Provincial Park.

Mile 122 GISCOME

On the edge of the McGregor Plateau lie three small lakes *(mile 105-121)* named Hansard, Aleza and Eaglet. For almost 60 years they were full of log booms waiting to be sent to the mill at Giscome. The sawmill, which was one of the largest in British Columbia, closed in 1974, and, as had happened at other times in its past, Giscome returned to margins of history.

Giscome first rose to fame in 1863 because it was on the most direct route – the shortest portage – between the Fraser and Peace river systems, an important route for gold seekers. A trading post was built in 1873, but within 20 years it languished and the area became overgrown. At this point, the Arctic Divide, which separates the watersheds that drain either to the north or to the west, is relatively low.

Mile 146 PRINCE GEORGE

The *Skeena* enters Prince George on a graceful, scalloped steel bridge over the Fraser. The bridge was built in 1914 by the Grand Trunk Pacific Railway, with a movable span for stern-wheelers, but the arrival of the railroad quickly spelled the end of river traffic and the span was rarely used.

The great explorer Alexander Mackenzie passed by in 1793, but it was Simon Fraser who in 1807 sited a post here at the confluence of the Nechako and the Fraser. The two mighty rivers meet like the arms of a crude letter 'Y,' and the Fraser emerges from the juncture to continue south to the Pacific.

PROFILE

The unpopulated region the *Skeena* traverses to reach Prince George may give a false impression of the city's place in the province. In fact, it is the geographical centre of British Columbia and the crossroad of major north-south and east-west transportation routes.

Lumber is another reason for Prince George's existence, and the city pays homage to this major industry with the booster slogan "White Spruce Capital of the World." Prince George is home to 66,000 residents and is the third-largest city in the province. It is a centre of administration, distribution, education and entertainment for the entire north.

The city centre lies in 'the bowl,' a broad depression which was the bed of an ancient lake. The developed area continues up the gentle cut banks, or sandhills, that ring Prince George.

William Surgenor Collection

59

ALL ABOARD!

Mile 0 PRINCE GEORGE

The Carrier Sekani tribe who first lived in this region traded with the coastal native people centuries ago, and the route the *Skeena* travels retraces some westward expanse of the plateau. The diverse landscape includes huge ranches and rolling farmland in open country, extensive towering forests of spruce, pine and fir, and some of the largest natural lakes in British Columbia.

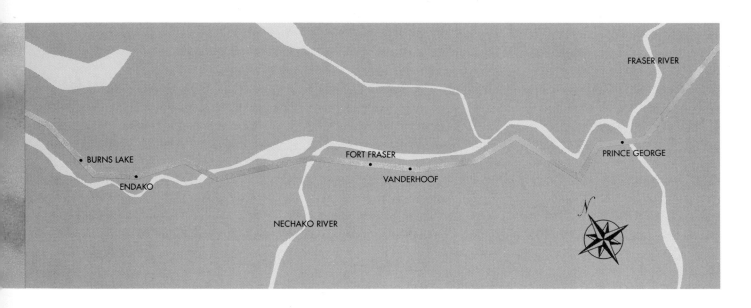

of their ancient paths over the broad Interior Plateau. The wide, rolling plateau cuts across the province from the Rocky Mountain Trench to the Coast Range, creating a breathing space between the parallel peaks of the Western Cordillera.

Leaving Prince George, the tracks follow the south bank of the Nechako River, climbing to reach the higher

Mile 69 VANDERHOOF

Vanderhoof (pop. 3,000) was named for an American public relations genius. Herbert Vanderhoof was hired by several railroad companies in the early 1900s to lure settlers to the Canadian west. He was so successful that the Grand Trunk Pacific's surveyors named this riverside townsite for him in 1914.

The wide surrounding valley is agricultural and includes grainfields, which are unusual for British Columbia. Vanderhoof is a busy service centre for ranchers and loggers, who stroll the streets in their cowboy boots and hard-hats. A bird sanctuary stretches five kilometres along the Nechako, and every spring and fall, about 50,000 Canada geese stop to rest during their migration.

Mile 94 FORT FRASER

This community (pop. 400) marks the departure of the Nechako as it turns south, and the *Skeena* crosses the river to travel alongside Fraser Lake. The tracks bisect Beaumont Provincial Park, the site of the original Fort Fraser, founded by the explorer Simon Fraser.

The reddish hills on the north shore of the lake take their colour from the 25-million-year-old lava flows of Table Mountain, the flat-topped remnants of its volcanic cone visible to the northwest. At the west end of the lake *(mile 107)* is the attractive lakeside town of Fraser Lake (pop. 1,200). The train bridges the Stellako River *(mile 109)* which, at only eight kilometres, is the shortest river in British Columbia.

The region from Endako to Smithers is prime moose country. In fact, most of this species in the province are found in central British Columbia. In winter, the moose make their feeding ground in swampy areas where patches of willows grow; in summer, deer are seen.

Mile 35 BURNS LAKE

The *Skeena* crosses the winding Endako River eight times *(mile 10-21)* before reaching the northern shoreline of long, thin Burns Lake. The town of Burns Lake (pop. 1,700) is an access point to Tweedsmuir Provincial Park, the greatest wilderness park in British Columbia, accessible only by boat or float-plane. Burns Lake is a resort centre for the province's Lakes District, known for its extravagance of fishing spots.

Geologically, the Burns Lake area is unusual. A huge boulder containing fossils, found in 1986, is displayed in the Lakes District Museum. Just south of the lake are the Eagle Creek opal deposits, one of the few places these rare precious stones can be found in Western Canada. Rockhounds also hunt for the more common white, amber and green agates.

Mile 115 ENDAKO

Endako (pop. 99) is another *Railway Division Point*, where the miles again begin to be counted from '0.' The Endako Molybdenum Mine claims to be the largest producer in the world of this silver-white metallic element, used for the hardening of steel.

Mile 51 ROSE LAKE

There aren't any roses in this small lake, but its unusual waters flow two ways, east to the Fraser River and west to the Bulkley River where the Skeena River system originates. There are hundreds of lakes between Burns Lake and Prince Rupert, and they act like magnets to fly-fishermen from all over the world. One spot has earned the name "Millionaires' Pool" because Bob Hope and other representatives of the rich and famous have visited.

Graceful, soaring bald eagles are frequently seen here and along the rest of the *Skeena's* route. British Columbia is home to one-fourth of the world's bald eagle population.

Mile 85 HOUSTON

En route to Houston (pop. 3,300), the *Skeena* crosses the twisting Bulkley River 11 times. Houston was named for pioneer newspaperman John Houston, who arrived in 1910 when the town was called Pleasant Valley.

This community is located where the Morice River joins the Bulkley. The two rivers give Houston its distinction as "Steelhead Capital." Resource industries such as logging, large sawmills and a silver mine keep Houston prosperous.

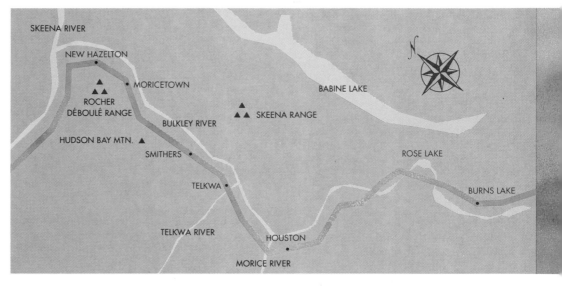

SKEENA RIVER
NEW HAZELTON
MORICETOWN
ROCHER DÉBOULÉ RANGE
BULKLEY RIVER
HUDSON BAY MTN.
SMITHERS
TELKWA
TELKWA RIVER
HOUSTON
MORICE RIVER
SKEENA RANGE
BABINE LAKE
ROSE LAKE
BURNS LAKE

Mile 116 TELKWA

The train heads north along the Bulkley Valley through a lightly forested area containing mostly aspen trees. The village of Telkwa (pop. 900) was the hub of the valley at the turn of the century.

The dramatic simplicity of 90-year-

old St. Stephen's church definitely makes it a heritage building in this young province.

The community got its start in 1865 when the Collins Overland Telegraph attempted to link America and Europe via Siberia. Though the telegraph line was made unnecessary by the Atlantic cable and was never finished, it was a significant accomplishment.

Mile 125 SMITHERS

Entering Smithers, the *Skeena* passes through a large sawmill yard with neatly stacked lumber and logs piled on both sides of the tracks. Smithers (pop. 5,000) is in the middle of the Bulkley Valley, a region rich in the history of both the native peoples and European pioneers. There are ghost towns, totem poles and Chinese graves.

Smithers marks the end of the Interior Plateau and is surrounded by four mountain ranges: the Babine, Hazelton, Telkwa and Omineca. It is becoming a winter resort known for the challenging skiing available on Hudson Bay Mountain. Recreation options include hunting, thanks to a healthy population of moose, mule deer, grizzly bears, mountain goats and caribou. This prosperous town is a service centre for the valley's resource industries and is a *Railway Division Point*, from which the mileage is numbered from '0.'

ALL ABOARD!

Mile 0 SMITHERS

Leaving Smithers, the *Skeena* enjoys expansive views of Hudson Bay Mountain to the south, and Kathlyn Lake to the north *(mile 4-5)*. Mountains can be seen all along the *Skeena's* route, but none are as dominant as Hudson Bay (2,621 metres), looming alone over the landscape. On this distinctive peak nestles the Kathlyn Glacier, an ice cirque more than 100 metres thick. The glacier drains through the picturesque 152-metre Twin Falls, down the rocky walls of two-kilometre-wide Glacier Gulch.

Mile 22 MORICETOWN

The village of the Carrier tribe at Moricetown (pop. 680) is called "Kyah

Glenbow Archives, Calgary

Wiget," and is the oldest settlement in the Bulkley Valley. People have been catching spring salmon here for 5,000 years, using spear-like gaffs to pluck the milling fish from the rapids.

Small farms dot the valley where the land is flat and arable. At Porphyry Creek *(mile 31)* the long curve of the 77-metre-long trestle offers passengers an opportunity to take photographs of the front of the sleek, stainless steel *Skeena* from the rear cars.

The bottom of the green-forested valley changes to the slick rock sides of the Bulkley Canyon *(mile 38)*. Three tunnels run through the canyon, including one of the longest (630 metres) used by passenger trains in Canada. The Bulkley Gate *(mile 41)* is a wall of rock that juts into the river.

Mile 45 NEW HAZELTON

At New Hazelton (pop. 850) the *Skeena* train meets its namesake river for the first time. The tracks describe a large southwest arc, dropping in elevation to follow the "river of mists" all the way to the Pacific.

home along the Skeena River and are linked within the Tsimshian language group and its art forms. The art of the Tsimshian, especially their carvings, is greatly admired. Paintings on canoes and totem poles create a dramatic effect. Usually, the carvings and paintings

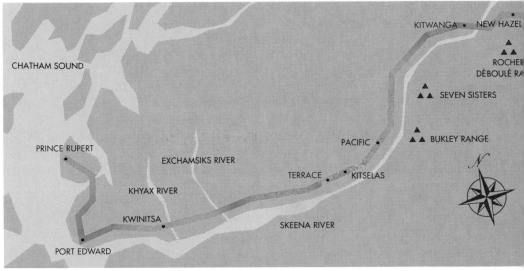

The three communities known as the Hazeltons (area pop. 2,000) are collectively called the "Totem Pole Capital of the World," and a few examples are visible from the train between here and Prince Rupert. Hazelton is the heartland of the rich culture of the Tsimshian, Kitsumkalum and Gitksan peoples, who make their

depict supernatural beings.

The 275-metre-long Sealy Gulch Bridge *(mile 50)* gives an expansive view of the meeting place where the Skeena and Bulkley valleys connect. The bold rock face of Rocher Déboulé (2,514 metres), also called "the mountain of rolling stone," rises suddenly and dramatically to the south.

Mile 73 KITWANGA

Many place-names in the region begin with the syllable Kit (or Git), which means "People of..." in the Tsimshian language. Kitwanga (pop. 400) translates as "People of the place of the rabbits."

Emily Carr, the doyen of Canadian artists, often sketched the totem poles of Kitwanga. Her native Indian name was Klee Wyck, "the laughing one." Most of the community lies beyond the hill, but one totem pole is beside the tracks, on the south side.

When the mists lift from the valley of the Skeena River, the stunning peaks of the surrounding mountains are revealed. The Seven Sisters *(mile 74-100)* march in a dramatic file to the south, though only six peaks are identifiable (the seventh stands in front).

Mile 107 PACIFIC

This abandoned townsite is notorious for the bears attracted to its berry flats during the summer, and 20 or more might be seen as the *Skeena* rolls west to Terrace. At this point, in early fall, mushroom pickers gather pine mushrooms for export to the world's restaurants. Usk *(mile 119)* is easily

recognized by the orange-and-white towers of its reaction ferry, moving cars and people across the waters of the Skeena River and using only the force of the current for power.

Mile 121 KITSELAS CANYON

The mouth of this three-kilometre canyon is broken up by jagged rock outcroppings that look like the teeth in a comb. The rapids flowing through its narrow gaps made it an enormous hazard for the stern-wheelers that plied the river from Prince Rupert to Hazelton at the turn of the century. Captains of the vessels would run cables through rings embedded in the sides of the canyon and winch the flat-bottomed boats through.

Here, the mountains have their feet in the river, and the railroaders were forced to tunnel through in four places. Between tunnels, there's a good view of the mouth of the Kitselas.

Mile 131 TERRACE

Terrace (pop. 11,000) gets its name from the landscape; the changing course of the river has cut terraced levels in the sides of the Kitsumkalum Valley. The city's symbol is a unique bear called the Kermodei that makes its habitat nearby. It's a subspecies of the black bear, whose fur can range from dark blond to gray, and is protected from hunters.

Terrace is at another *Railway Division Point*, from which the miles are counted from '0.' West of Terrace, the Skeena widens, and is divided into channels by islands and sandbars. Major rivers enter the Skeena from the north, including the Exstew *(mile 24)*, the Exchamsiks *(mile 35)*, and the Kasiks *(mile 39)*. All of the tributary mouths are noted fishing spots and many were the sites of gold sluicing operations during the Omineca Rush of the 1870s.

`Mile 48` KWINITSA

The rock bluffs of Kwinitsa host more than 50 waterfalls in season, the most enduring of which is the vertical gully of the 450-metre Emanon Falls *(mile 46)*. The area is a dangerous slide zone, with snow in winter and falling rock in summer. The forested peaks of the Coast Range high above are scarred by slide chutes.

Waves in the river hint that the Skeena is influenced by the tides, though at this point, the Pacific Ocean is still almost 60 kilometres away.

`Mile 60` KHYAX RIVER

The estuary portion of the Skeena River is the site of tremendous runs by salmon and small oolichan fish. Here the water is often crowded with fishing boats and a white cloud of birds hovers above. Oolichan are a source of edible oil, and during the March run, gigantic sea lions

will chase the fish well up the river. The coastal tribes traded this valuable oil with the interior people, and their ancient paths, frequently called the "grease trail," took much the same route as the *Skeena* does today.

The mouth of the Khyax marks the start of "Cannery Row." Only the pilings standing along the river, marking templates of docks and piers, are a clue to the former importance of the canneries to the region. Thousands of native Indian, Chinese and Japanese workers would spend the season in dormitory villages built over the water. The few remaining buildings are in ruins, except for the restored 1889 North Pacific Cannery at Port Edward *(mile 86)*.

`Mile 94` PRINCE RUPERT

Ridley Island *(mile 87)* was developed in the 1980s, providing coal and grain shipping terminals of major importance to the north coast. The train has left the Skeena River and crosses over the Zenardi Rapids to Kaien Island and the end of the line.

Prince Rupert (pop. 16,000) hugs the northern edge of the 11-kilometre-long island, which has two 600-metre

peaks. The dominant mountain, with an aerial tram, is called Mt. Hays, after the president of the railway company which developed the port. Charles Melville Hays, who is remembered in many other place-names in Western Canada, died in the sinking of the Titanic in 1912 before the planning of Prince Rupert was completed.

Named after the first governor of the Hudson's Bay Company, Prince Rupert, which bills itself as "The Halibut Capital of the World," is a mere 64 kilometres south of the Alaska border. It's a port for cruise ships heading to Alaska and for British Columbia Ferry Corporation sailings through the scenic Inside Passage to Vancouver Island. Ferries also take travellers to the Queen Charlotte Islands, the scenic homeland of the Haida people.

Though it rains often and heavily, when the weather is good, Prince Rupert is a fine place for walking along the waterfront, past its several fish canneries, ships' chandlers and colourful fishing boats. For an indoor pastime, the top attraction is the Museum of Northern British Columbia, with an excellent collection of modern aboriginal art of the region, artifacts as old as 10,000 years and a totem pole carving shed.

"The Great Sea

Has set me adrift,

It moves me as the weed in the river,

Earth and the great weather

Move me,

And move my inward parts with joy."

Uvavnuk's trance song

HUDSON BAY

The name Hudson Bay sparks the imagination with romantic images and historical perspectives. Henry Hudson's notorious voyage in 1610 was an attempt to find the elusive Northwest Passage to the Orient. Instead, his crew mutinied and the explorer was set adrift at the south end of the bay. Hudson never did find the passage but both the river and bay bear his name.

The region proved to be cruel for the early fur traders who during the 1700 and 1800s had to contend with the ice-bound sea and the desolation of the barren land. The natural grandeur of the region still guards its mysterious side. Today, VIA serves this northern region, tracing a 1,700-kilometre path from Winnipeg to Churchill.

The *Hudson Bay* journey begins at the elegant Union Station in Winnipeg and travels to Churchill Station. Along the way, the trackside scenery changes from the fertile Prairie heartlands to the immense forests of the Canadian Shield. Finally, the train windows frame the subtle beauty of the tundra meeting the blue expanse of the deep sea.

From October through April, the Northern Lights are at their brightest.

ALL ABOARD!

Mile 0 WINNIPEG

Winnipeg is the starting point of the *Hudson Bay* journey, and the approximate mid-point of VIA's premier service, aboard the transcontinental *Canadian*,

which runs between Vancouver and Toronto. *(For information about Manitoba, a description of Winnipeg and the start of the Hudson Bay's route, please read pages 20 to 22.)*

Mile 55 PORTAGE LA PRAIRIE

The *Hudson Bay* departs from the tracks it has been sharing with the

Canadian and makes a loop westward into the province of Saskatchewan before heading into the rugged and lightly populated north.

Eastward is Lake Manitoba, whose wetlands are one of the largest waterfowl staging areas in North America.

Mile 121 DAUPHIN

Dauphin (pop. 8,875) is in the lush valley between Riding Mountain and Duck Lake Provincial Parks, on the banks of the Vermilion River. The town has both historic and cultural importance. The explorer La Vérendrye discovered

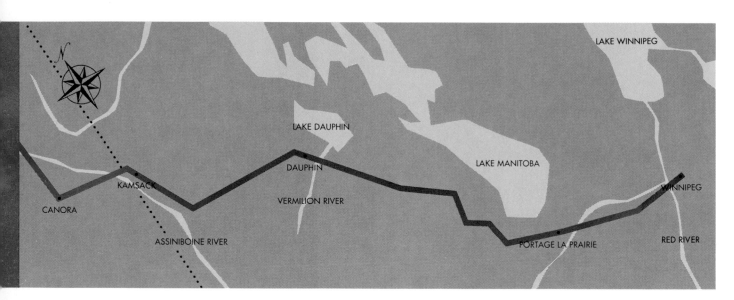

Continuing west, the train skirts Riding Mountain National Park, covering almost 3,000 square kilometres of boreal and deciduous forests, aspen parkland and open grassland. The park is home to bison and a rich collection of animal and bird life.

Lake Dauphin in 1739 and established the fur trading outpost of Fort Dauphin not far from the current townsite.

Dauphin is a centre of Ukrainian settlement in Canada, and the home of Canada's National Ukrainian Festival. From 1896 to 1925, Ukrainian settlers and immigrants from Russia were instrumental in the agricultural development of the Prairies. Many communities along this portion of the *Hudson Bay's* route give a clue to their ethnic origins in the onion-domed style of their churches.

Leaving Dauphin, the *Hudson Bay* travels northwest, crossing the Vermilion as the train leaves town. Dauphin is a *Railway Division Point*, from which the mileposts are again numbered from '0.'

Mile 100 KAMSACK

The *Hudson Bay* travels through rolling terrain with thickly wooded hills en route to Kamsack. This Saskatchewan community (pop. 2,565) is a key place in the history of the meetings of the native peoples and Europeans. The area is the traditional home of the Saulteaux band, who signed a treaty with the Dominion of Canada in 1874.

The Assiniboine River, a bit west of Kamsack, was a fur trading route. Several trading posts were built in the area, the first in 1793 and the last operating until 1912. The North West Mounted Police (forerunners of the famed Mounties) also built a fort nearby in 1874.

The aspen-covered hills rising gradually to the west are the eastern part of Duck Mountain Provincial Park. Turkey vultures live in the park, and moose, white-tailed deer and beaver are particularly plentiful.

Mile 124 CANORA

Canora (pop. 2,500) is another town enhanced with reminders of "the old country," as in the typical Kiev architecture of the Ukrainian Orthodox Heritage Church. Hardy European settlers broke the first fields and farmland in this region, and their descendants are represented in the 10 ethno-cultural groups in Canora's annual summer Multicultural Festival. Northward, the *Hudson Bay* moves from parklands to pine into a sparsely populated region. Far to the west rise the Porcupine Hills, a recreation area of lakes and campgrounds. Canora is a *Railway Division Point*.

Mile 93 HUDSON BAY

The train is 1,000 kilometres from the icy waters of the bay, but this Saskatchewan community commemorates its place as a link in the chain the fur traders welded between their port and the trapping lands. Hudson Bay (pop. 2,200)

Vancouver Public Library

was originally called Etomami, a native Indian word meaning "three rivers joined together." The *Hudson Bay* meets the Etomami River coming into town, crosses the Red Deer River running west to east, and leaves with the Fir River.

Historically the four themes of the town, recreated in the circa 1905 heritage park, are railway, logging, farming and fur trading. Today Hudson Bay is also a recreational centre. Wildcat Hills Wilderness Area is 20 kilometres north, characterized by steep canyons and fast flowing rivers. Wildlife includes moose, bear, lynx, deer and wolves. Hudson Bay is a *Railway Division Point*.

Mile 88 THE PAS

The name The Pas comes either from the native Indian word Opasquiaow, meaning "water converging to a narrows with spruce-treed highlands," or from the French for "narrow passage." The large Saskatchewan River and the much smaller Pasquia River meet here.

The Pas (pop. 6,600) is one of the oldest communities in Manitoba, a traditional meeting point between Hudson Bay and the south. Arctic explorer Sir John Franklin gave the settlement a sun dial in 1842. (The Franklin expedition went missing in 1845 while searching for the North West Passage and, by 1848, all members were dead. A search party carved furniture for the church in The Pas during the winter of 1846.) The town's Trappers' Festival, founded in 1916, is Canada's oldest winter event.

The Pas lies "north of 53," the

parallel that marked the provincial boundary until 1881. The landscape includes evergreen forests covering thousands of square kilometres, many lakes and rivers. Continuing on its journey, the *Hudson Bay* passes Clearwater Lake Provincial Park and its unique 'caves,' a phenomenon formed by huge slabs that have broken away from dolomite cliffs. For approximately the next 145 kilometres, limestone formations punctuate the landscape with their unique appearance.

To the west, Cormorant Lake *(mile 31)* is the centre of the Cormorant Provincial Forest, and is the setting for a bird sanctuary and the lakeshore community of Cormorant *(mile 41)*.

Mile 81 WEKUSKO

Wekusko (pop. 51) is a Cree word meaning "herb lake." Soon after passing Wekusko, the landscape changes from limestone to muskeg.

Wabowden (pop. 284), is set in rolling countryside *(mile 136)*. Part of this region was former lake bed, and Wabowden nestles on the shores of beautiful Bowden Lake. To the east lies Rock Island Lake.

Mile 191 THOMPSON JUNCTION

At this point, a 49-kilometre rail line branches west to Thompson (pop. 15,000), site of the INCO nickel mine, called the "Hub of the North." The planned city was built in the 1950s after discovery of the world's second-largest nickel deposits, and today Thompson is an oasis of suburbia surrounded by wilderness.

The Pikwitonei River connects Pikwitonei Lake to the east of the track, with Cook Lake to the west *(mile 213)*. The *Hudson Bay* makes its first crossing of Nelson River at Manitou Rapids, a narrow channel that carries waters originating in the English, Winnipeg, Red, Assiniboine, North and South Saskatchewan rivers *(mile 240)*.

Mile 326 GILLAM

The land is flat, with plenty of muskeg and few trees, as the train begins to leave the Pre-Cambrian rock of the Canadian Shield's Laurentian Plateau *(mile 319)*. Ahead lies the wet, coastal plain of the Hudson Bay Lowlands. The shifting soil of the permafrost, which extends 12 metres into the ground, means that communication lines must be

track. Below the dam lie the Kettle Rapids, where the *Hudson Bay* crosses the Nelson River again *(mile 331)*.

At Amery, the train turns sharply north and heads straight for Churchill *(mile 355)*.

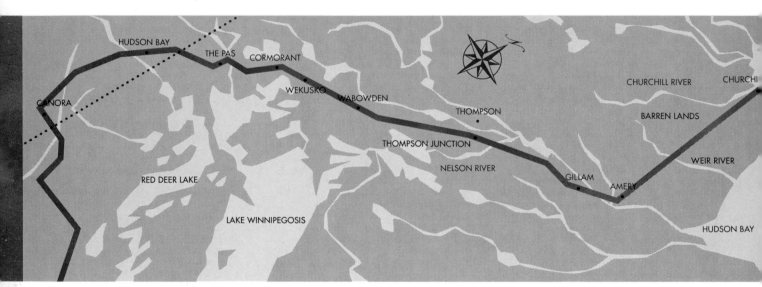

supported on tripods. Gillam (pop. 1,900) grew from a tiny community to a significant town thanks to hydroelectric development. It is situated on the gigantic Nelson River between the three generating stations at Long Spruce, Kettle, and Limestone. The dam for these important hydroelectric projects created Stephens Lake to the west of the railway

Mile 440 BARREN LANDS

The tundra landscape north of the treeline is called the Barren Lands, though it actually supports a great deal of wildlife. Arctic ptarmigan, unlike other grouse, can change the colour of their feathers for seasonal camouflage, and are abundant around the Weir River crossing *(mile 373)*. Red, white and silver fox can

often be spotted in the wild. During the short, intense summer a huge variety of wildflowers carpets the soil, and includes the pink Indian paintbrush, white Labrador tea and red Arctic sweet pea. In fall, soapberry and the scarlet bearberry are prevalent, along with the delicate Arctic avens.

Deer River follows the track on the west, finally joining the wide Churchill River, which runs into Hudson Bay. The powerful tides of the bay push into the mouth of the river and force its waters back upstream, making a distinct, visible boundary where salt and fresh water meet. Local boatmen can straddle this line and taste the different waters on each side of their boats.

Mile 509 CHURCHILL

For at least 4,000 years, people have travelled through this area, establishing camps where the Churchill River flows into the bay. Over the last 400 years, since the arrival of Europeans, Churchill has been a trading post, British fort, astronomical observatory, rocket range and military installation. With the completion of the railway line in 1929, the community reached its present

incarnation as deep-sea port and grain-handling facility.

The Danish sailor Jens Munck is credited with the discovery of Churchill Harbour in 1619. All his crew except two died on its shores, yet he managed to sail back to Denmark. (Explorer Henry Hudson also had bad luck. He gave his name to the huge bay in 1610, but his crew mutinied and cast him adrift.)

The Hudson's Bay Company started a fort at Churchill in 1688, constructed of stone walls 12 metres thick that took 40 years to complete. The impressive Prince of Wales Fort can be visited during the *Hudson Bay's* layover in Churchill. It stands just across from the harbour entrance, restored to its original condition, with several cannon still in position.

PROFILE

Churchill (pop. 1,200) is on solid land on the rocky coast of Hudson Bay, but is surrounded by oceans of water and bog. The townsite is a thin strip of land at the bottleneck-shaped mouth of the Churchill River; the harbour is excellent, with a deep river channel averaging 16 metres. Barley and wheat are shipped

Vancouver Public Library

from Churchill, which becomes a busy port in its short shipping season from late July to late October.

Churchill is like a convention centre for polar bears, who boost the economy by attracting their weight in tourists. Hundreds of bears gather every autumn in the Cape Churchill area, 64 kilometres from town, where they wait for the bay to freeze so they can cross the ice to hunt seals. Nearer the city lies a denning area where female bears retire to cub. Bears often wander the city streets in season, requiring safety patrols and bear alert drills in the schools.

Also white but far less dangerous, Beluga whales frequent the Churchill River in thousands. They feed in the rich fishing grounds and calve in the warmer water, their white bodies clearly visible in the blue water as they swim and surface. The belugas are protected after overhunting seriously reduced their population, and now whale-watching boats are a popular tourist pastime.

Other highlights at the end of the *Hudson Bay's* journey celebrate the aboriginal culture of the Inuit and Dene tribes who have thrived in this wilderness region for thousands of years. The Eskimo Museum features exhibits depicting Inuit history and contemporary Inuit art.

Traditional Arctic lifestyles of hunting and trapping are part of everyday life for many Churchill residents.

Soon the *Hudson Bay* will arrive at its destination, but just as the radiance of the Northern Lights bathes the sky in colour, the memories of this journey will continue to dazzle the mind.

These lights inspired Inuit tribes to believe in legends that told of spirits carrying torches to guide souls on their final journey. According to the Dene people, these "spiritwalkers" will come at a whistle and a clap, to fulfill wishes. It's a pleasant thought to carry as the *Hudson Bay* returns southward, rolling beneath the vivid skies.

"Athwart the beauty and the breast

Of purpling airs they twirl and twist,

Then float away to some far rest,

Leaving the skies all colour-kiss't –

A glorious and a golden West

That greets the Lifting of the Mist."

E. Pauline Johnson from "The Lifting of the Mist"

Malahat

VIA Rail's *Malahat* Dayliner train travels Canada's westernmost passenger route, running 225 kilometres along the coast of Vancouver Island, from Victoria on the island's southern tip to the mid-island community of Courtenay.

The line is still known to many people as the Esquimalt and Nanaimo Railway – or E & N – because it was built between the former's harbour and the latter's coal seams. The railway was vital to the development of Vancouver Island's economy and population growth, and knitted together the settlements that quickly sprung up along the route.

Steam locomotives have given way to RDCs – self-propelled rail diesel cars that don't need a locomotive unit – but the contrast and grandeur of Vancouver Island scenery has not changed. As the *Malahat* leaves Victoria behind, travellers are introduced to the pastoral side of the island, with plenty of parkland, small fishing communities, and farms where sheep, cattle and horses can be seen grazing in the fields. Never far away is the forested wilderness, home to eagles, bears and elk. Here, a more gentle lifestyle thrives along with plenty of spacious parkland.

VANCOUVER ISLAND

Vancouver Island is the largest North American island in the Pacific, a bastion off the coast of British Columbia that protects the mainland from ocean storms. Its 3,440-kilometre coastline is endlessly serrated with inlets and

harbours, and fringed with an abundance of smaller isles, particularly the Gulf Islands that lie in the narrow Strait of Georgia between Vancouver Island and the mainland.

"The island," as it's called locally, was named for Captain George Vancouver of Britain's Royal Navy, who circumnavigated its shores during his surveys of the North American coast in 1792. Like most visitors, he was charmed by the island and wrote:

"The serenity of the climate, the innumerable pleasing landscapes, and the abundant fertility that nature puts forth, require only to be enriched by the industry of man with villages, mansions, cottages and other buildings, to render it the most lovely country that can be imagined."

The industry of people has indeed shaped the island, mining it for coal and gold, logging it for valuable timber, and establishing the provincial capital city, Victoria. However, most of Vancouver Island remains a rugged wilderness close to the natural wonders that support its resource industries and attract tourists. From mid-March through to mid-April, whale watchers gather for the gray whale migration. There are often sightings of humpback and finback whales, and occasionally, the rare sperm whale makes an appearance.

A mountainous spine runs its length, only to break up into long mountain fjords on a wild, west coast that cuts deeply into the island. The gentler east coast lies in the mountains' rainshadow.

VICTORIA

One of those "other buildings" Captain Vancouver dreamed of is the Provincial Legislature building, symbol of Victoria's status as the capital of British Columbia. On its green copper dome stands a gilded statue of Captain Vancouver, gazing over the city he literally put on the map. The Legislature, and the world-famous Empress Hotel nearby, are on the Inner Harbour, which was the city's original raison d'être.

Victoria (pop. 285,000) began its life in 1843 as a port for the fur trade, under the aegis of the Hudson's Bay Company, which at one time ruled the island and paid rent of only seven shillings a year. The 1858 gold rush on the mainland transformed Fort Victoria into a thriving commercial and government centre. A steadily increasing number of settlers looked inland to the mineral and lumber resources that have been the mainstays of the economy ever since.

Much like the queen it is named after, Victoria has a reputation for old-fashioned English respectability. Both residents and visitors take afternoon tea and ride red double-decker buses, and

lawn bowling and cricket are popular. But Victoria comes with a multicultural twist that is all-Canadian. City landmarks include the ornate Gate of Harmonious Interest in Chinatown and the grandeur of the totem poles carved by the Cowichan, Sooke and Salish peoples.

remnants of its colourful past. The station itself was built in 1985 and contains two striking stained glass windows depicting early rail scenes.

The station anchors one end of the bright blue Johnston St. Bridge, which marks the division between the Inner

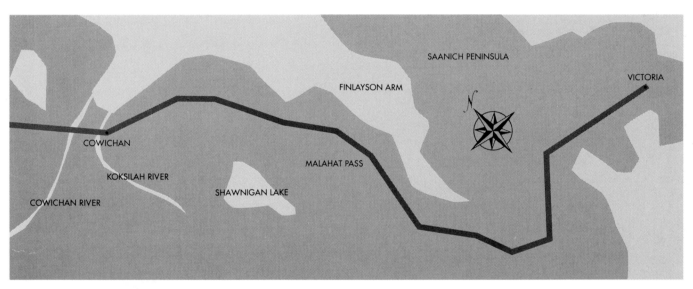

ALL ABOARD!

Mile 0 VICTORIA

Victoria Station sits at the edge of the redeveloped old city, among some of Victoria's most interesting heritage buildings. A huge whale mural across the street is a sign of the modern vitality that Victoria displays alongside the historic

Harbour with its tourist attractions, and the Upper Harbour with its working fishing boats. At night, the 3,000 tiny white light bulbs that frame the Legislature Building create an oft-photographed image that sheds light on the Inner Harbour.

Leaving Victoria Station, the *Malahat* passes the back streets of the

city, through alternating belts of industrial and residential neighbourhoods. Many of these streets cross the railway tracks, requiring the train to sound its whistle almost constantly.

the Canadian Coast Guard.

The waters of Esquimalt Harbour are to the west; nearer, and to the east of the tracks, is Portage Inlet, its calm waters ringed by green lawns and homes. The marshes along the waterway are the habitat of many birds, and blue heron, cormorants, cranes and swans are commonly sighted. Already the *Malahat* has passed through rock-cuts that signal the rugged terrain to come, as a distant line of hills approaches. Langford Lake and a suburb bearing the same name lie to the west *(mile 8)*.

Mile 12 GOLDSTREAM PROV. PARK

This significant expanse of wilderness was named for its false Eldorado of 1885. Mineshafts can still be found; they once produced small quantities of gold, and some people still pan the Goldstream River. In October and November the river is full of spawning salmon. Rock-faces interrupt the lush greenery of ferns, wildflowers and the flowering dogwood that is the provincial emblem. In the park are groves of 600-year-old Douglas firs, western red cedar, and many trees coloured silver and lime-green with lichen and moss.

Mile 4 ESQUIMALT

The suburbs of Victoria include Esquimalt, a Canadian Forces dockyard that provides a direct link to the days of Captain George Vancouver, who noted its deep harbour as a potential naval base. Under large cranes can be seen various vessels being refitted and repaired, including the bright orange icebreakers of

The train begins climbing through its namesake Malahat Range, which is cut by deep gorges and bridged with dramatic trestles at Niagara Canyon *(mile 14)* and Arbutus Canyon *(mile 14.9).* Passengers afraid of heights should sit on the west side of the cars, and those who like gazing over sheer drops, on the east side! Niagara was named for a falls over which rushes a ribbon of white water 79 metres below the train; Arbutus for the trees with peeling orange-red bark and silvery foliage that can be spotted 73 metres below, and elsewhere along the line. There is only one tunnel on the *Malahat's* journey *(mile 15).*

Mile 20 MALAHAT PASS

The blue reach of Finlayson Arm cuts deep into Vancouver Island. The Saanich Peninsula is to the east *(mile 16-18).* The view encompasses several Gulf Islands, and on a clear day the distant white cone of Mt. Baker (3,285 metres) is visible 121 kilometres eastward in Washington State.

Malahat Pass (elev. 278 metres) is the highest point on the route *(mile 20).* Descending, the train offers a glimpse of two small lakes to the west before reaching the largest lake on the route, Shawnigan Lake *(mile 23).* The tracks wind along the shore of the eight-kilometre-long lake, a well-established summer vacation area, past docks and beaches, old cottages and new houses.

After Shawnigan, the landscape evolves into farmland, with cow trails winding through the trees. The picturesque farming community of Cobble Hill is part of the rural area population of 10,000 *(mile 30).*

Mile 35 COWICHAN

To the west, across the street from the station in the community of Cowichan Bay (pop. 3,300) is a quaint country church surrounded by thick trimmed hedges, like a bit of Olde England. The name of this region is the Anglicized native Indian word "Khowutzun," meaning "basking in the sun" or "the warm land."

The Cowichan is British Columbia's largest band of native people (pop. 2,200), belonging to the Coast Salish tribe, and is famed for making garments of black, grey and off-white wool. For centuries, they've used spears to take salmon from the Cowichan River runs.

William Surgenor Collection

The Koksilah River *(mile 37)* is the prelude to the Cowichan River *(mile 39).* It's an unassuming but fast, rocky stream at this point. The Cowichan flows 64 kilometres from its headwaters in Lake Cowichan, through forests and canyons, before finally reaching its estuary and

As the native people have known since long before the arrival of Europeans, the river has major runs of chinook, coho and chum salmon, and it is the native peoples' tradition to offer the first fish that appears each year to an eagle, which represents the legendary Thunderbird.

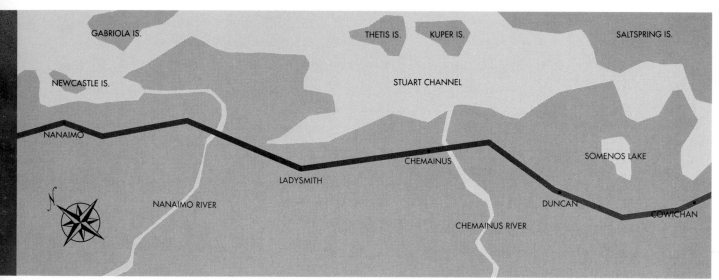

then spilling through fertile fields.

It is a mecca for anglers and remains one of the province's best and most consistent producers, despite being one of its most heavily fished streams. The Cowichan River holds the rare-in-British Columbia brown trout, as well as the common rainbow and cutthroat, steelhead, kokanee and Dolly Varden.

Mile 40 DUNCAN

The town of Duncan (pop. 4,000) is the centre of the Cowichan Valley and the largest congregation of the area's population of 20,000. Duncan's claim to fame is its collection of 60 cedar totem poles, old and new. Thunderbirds and other symbols show that the native peoples' culture is alive and well in

Duncan. Many of the totems have been carved in the city, including the world's largest in diameter (over two metres), erected in 1988. There's an interesting cluster at the south end of the station. At the north end of the station, a red caboose is a reminder of the railway's history. The station is one of Duncan's heritage buildings and houses the Cowichan Valley Museum.

Somenos Lake, east of the station, floods in the winter to create large marshes that birds find attractive. Year-round, the flats attract waterfowl, as well as shorebirds in April and May, including ducks, Canada geese and swans. Several breeds of wild swans, including the rare trumpeter and whistling swan, migrate along the British Columbia coast.

Southwest of Duncan, the slopes of Waterloo Mountain are home to some of the oldest living trees in Canada – a grove of Douglas firs that sprouted after a massive forest fire 1,350 years ago.

Mile 50 CHEMAINUS

Farm country broadens into the Westholme Valley *(mile 42-48)*. An unusual turreted house stands above a seasonal lake on the eastern hills, from which rises Mt. Richards (311 metres). To the west are Mts. Prevost and Sicker, whose copper mines were once among the largest in the province. The area is dotted with ghost towns that teetered on the brink of prosperity before the mines were closed. The train may flush a bouquet of pheasants from the trackside bushes. The Chemainus River is crossed at *mile 47*.

Chemainus (pop. 4,000) owes its start to the logging industry, but today it's known as a major Canadian art centre. When the forest industry declined in 1982, Chemainus invited artists to paint large murals depicting the community's history. By the time the mill actually closed over the years 1983-1985, there were 12 murals, which became the core of a revitalization project that played a major role in boosting the town's finances.

New murals are added each year, painted by internationally recognized artists, and 30 were in place by the project's 10th anniversary, in 1992. An outdoor art gallery supported by shops and cafés attracts more than 300,000 visitors annually.

Offshore, across Stuart Channel, lie two of the Gulf Islands: Thetis, a recreation area and holiday resort, and Kruper, which contains both an Indian reserve and private land.

Mile 56 LADYSMITH

Ladysmith (pop. 4,400) is on the 49th Parallel, the boundary that also marks most of the world's longest undefended border, between Canada and the United States. But in the case of Vancouver Island, that border was pushed south to keep all the island within Canada. (The border threads its way through the Gulf Islands; those lying on the American side are known as the San Juan Islands.)

Ladysmith was named in 1899 for the South African city whose Boer War siege was lifted while this British Columbia site was being surveyed.

Ladysmith owes not only its name, but also its existence, to the Dunsmuir family. Robert Dunsmuir was a famous coal baron who built the E & N railway, and his son James created Ladysmith, originally as a private dock for coal shipments on Oyster Bay. Later, the miners' homes were transported from the pit head to create an instant town, one of Canada's first bedroom communities.

Ladysmith's coal era came to an abrupt end in the early 1930s when the seams became played out.

Timber was the next major industry and, recently, tourism has become a force in the local economy. The town has a fine collection of interesting historic buildings.

Mile 65 NANAIMO RIVER

The view from the *Malahat* as it crosses the Nanaimo River can be heart-stopping. Above and to the west, another bridge parallels the train's, and the bright ropes hanging over its side identify it as The Bungy Zone – where thrill-seekers bind their legs with giant rubber bands before leaping into space and swinging

over the river 42 metres below! Bungy jumping began in North America as something of a forbidden pleasure, banned by the authorities in many places but now legalized in British Columbia. The train stops if a jumper is ready to go, allowing passengers a perfect view.

Mile 73 NANAIMO

Nanaimo (pop. 59,700) is the third-oldest city in British Columbia. Long before incorporation, it was the site of five distinct native villages at a place called S'nenymo, meaning "great and mighty people" or "people of many names." The Spanish were there briefly in 1791, and the British a year later, but European involvement with Nanaimo didn't begin until coal was discovered in 1851.

Most of Nanaimo is downhill from the station, where a pleasant view stretches beyond the harbour to Newcastle Island, other Gulf Islands, the Coast Mountains on the mainland and cone-shaped Mt. Baker in Washington State. From January through April, the waters of the Nanaimo Harbour teem with the California and Stellar sea lions that come to feast on spawning herring. Cormorants, gulls and convocations of eagles can also be seen fishing.

An ecological reserve has been established southwest of Nanaimo to protect the Vancouver Island marmot. This cute brown rodent with white patches around its muzzle and forehead is about the size of a large house cat, and was first discovered in 1910. The marmot is found in Alpine meadows, and is an endangered species estimated to have a world population of only about 300, all in this area.

Mile 83 NANOOSE BAY

The train passes Diver Lake to the west, then Long Lake to the east. Green Lake follows, also to the west, and is the

most evident of the three *(mile 76-80)*.

Nanoose Bay is a protected harbour popular with windsurfers and sailors, and contains a large marina and resort at Schooner Cove. Nanoose is at times the centre of controversy, frequented as it is by the American nuclear submarines that

manila and silver mantles.

Yet another bridge crosses the Englishman River *(mile 92)*. The broad, rocky river is known for its dramatic falls, which drop 36.5 metres, and for petroglyphs (rock carvings), but these are not visible from the *Malahat*.

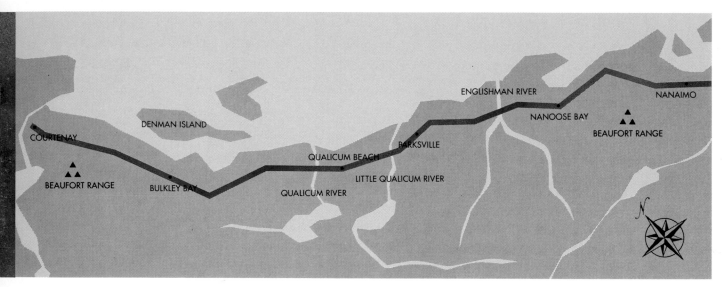

come to use an underwater weapons testing base.

The train leaves the shore briefly to cross a peninsula, then passes another cove, its sandy flats cut by streams. These waters and those to the north are the most intensive commercial oyster cultivating area in British Columbia. The clam population includes littleneck, butter,

Mile 94 PARKSVILLE

The northern part of the *Malahat's* route runs through the area known as the Beach Country, where long expanses of tidal sandflats attract clam diggers, beachcombers, and sand castle builders. At low tide, the beach seems to continue forever, and a chain of resorts extends to Qualicum Beach *(mile 101)*.

Parksville (pop. 7,000) is a well-established resort community and retirement centre. There are great views of the Strait of Georgia and the mountain ranges in the middle of the Island. The Parksville/Qualicum area is an important migration stopover for the Black Brant in March and April; other waterfowl frequent the area until October. Bald eagles are common and can be spotted in the high treetops or soaring over the waves, searching carefully for fish with their eagle eyes.

The train crosses a loop of French Creek on a 318-metre trestle over a gulch *(mile 98)*.

Mile 101 QUALICUM BEACH

This community (pop. 5,000) takes its name from an aboriginal word meaning "where the dog salmon run." Fishing has always been important here. The Little Qualicum River is good for rainbow and cutthroat trout, and steelhead *(mile 103)*. Upstream of the rail bridge there are falls dropping a total of 61 metres.

The Big Qualicum River is divided by a concrete 1,036-metre-long channel created to help spawning salmon, which

has drastically improved their survival rate. More than 100,000 fish return annually to the hatchery, which produces millions of little salmon *(mile 110)*.

Mile 110 DUNSMUIR

This stop on the banks of the Big Qualicum is named after the coal baron who was so critical to the development of this part of Vancouver Island. The Dunsmuirs were responsible for creating the E & N railway, for founding Ladysmith, Nanaimo and other communities, some of which are no longer in existence.

This northern portion of the *Malahat's* route is famous for its frequency of wildlife sightings. In the early spring, gangs of elk, often a dozen animals, can be seen in clear areas around Deep Bay *(mile 118)*. The trees are tall, which makes them popular with eagles. In summer, bears like to lie between the rails to bask in a sunny break from the surrounding forest.

Mile 126 BUCKLEY BAY

Near Buckley Bay, the train crosses several rivers, including Waterloo Creek *(mile 122)*. From the trestle over T'sable

River, a lovely view eastward frames Denman Island at the river's mouth *(mile 124)*. The resort community of Union Bay (pop. 100) *(mile 130)* has well-kept lawns and a view of Baynes Sound, between Vancouver Island and Denman Island.

Mile 139 COURTENAY

The *Malahat* enters the Comox Valley, marked by Denman Island on the east and extending west to the Beaufort Mountain Range. The landscape opens to vistas of the interior's snow-capped peaks (several of them topping 2,000 metres) and the Comox Glacier. The western peaks are part of the legendary Forbidden Plateau, so named by the Comox tribe after the women and children sent there for safety during a war raid disappeared without trace, perhaps taken by the gods. Together with Mt. Washington (1,649 metres) the plateau is Vancouver Island's busiest ski area.

The centre of the Valley is Courtenay (pop. 10,000), which was named for a captain of one of the British naval vessels that explored these waters. Its sister city Comox (pop. 7,600) contains a large Canadian Forces base. The cities are surrounded by the fertile

farmlands of the valley and offer fine views of mountains and islands. As with the other island communities, the region was developed by the Hudson's Bay Company, which persuaded settlers to establish farms in 1862.

Outdoor recreation is a major factor

in the Comox Valley economy. The mountains, rivers, farmland and beaches echo many of the memorable views that have been seen from the *Malahat* since leaving Victoria. Courtenay's charms make an appropriate end to the *Malahat's* journey, or a halfway marker for those travellers looking forward to the return trip.

P H O T O C R E D I T S

Bergen, Wes: Diarama; pages 22, 27, 40 (lower), 44 (lower), 45 (lower), 47, 61, 62, 65 (lower), 66 (lower), 67, 69 (upper), 75, 82, 85 (upper), 89, 94 (centre left).

Burda, Richard: Focus/Tony Stone; page 10.

Chapman, Fred: Diarama; pages 8, 12, 14 (upper), 23, 31, 37 (centre), 40 (upper), 43 (upper), 49, 56, 57 (right), 58, 86 (upper), 90 (right), 92, 93.

Edwards, John: Focus/Tony Stone; page 41.

Favrholdt, David: pages 9, 16 (lower), 18, 20, 26, 74 (lower).

Focus/Tony Stone: page 15 (right).

Hartley, Gordon: Diarama; page 29 (upper).

Ivy, Bill: Focus: page 15 (left).

Kozak, Myron: pages 57 (left), 63 (upper), 64 (upper), 68 (upper), 69 (lower), 70 (lower), 94 (upper).

Leighton, D: page 39 (lower).

Martell, Hugh: pages 13, 14 (lower), 16 (upper), 25 (left), 33 (lower), 36, 39 (upper), 77, 87, 95.

McDougall, Duncan: Diarama; pages 11 (upper), 45 (upper), 50, 54.

McDougall, Yvonne: Diarama; page 48.

McPhee, Don: Diarama; pages 60, 63 (lower), 68 (lower), 90 (left).

McPhee, Mildred: Focus/Tony Stone; page 64 (lower).

Miller, K.: Focus/Tony Stone; page 52 (left).

Piluke, N.: Focus/Tony Stone; page 11 (lower).

Talbot, Rob: Focus/Tony Stone; page 86 (centre).

Simpson, Richard: Focus/Tony Stone; inside back cover (right).

Warden, John: Focus/Tony Stone; page 37 (lower).

Alberta Tourism: pages 29 (lower), 33 (upper), 35, 55.

BC Tourism: pages 30 (lower), 42 (lower), 46 (upper & lower), 52 (right), 59, 66 (upper), 70 (upper), 83, 84, 86 (lower), 88, 94 (centre right), inside back cover (left).

Bungy Zone Co.: page 91 (upper).

Manitoba Tourism: pages 21 (upper), 72, 76, 79, 80 (lower).

VIA Rail Canada: inside front cover, pages 4, 5, 6 (upper and lower), 19 (right), 21 (lower), 24, 25 (right), 28, 30 (upper), 34, 37 (upper), 42 (upper), 43 (lower), 44 (upper), 51, 65 (upper), 73, 74 (upper), 78, 80 (upper), 85 (lower), 91 (lower), 98, 99, inside back cover (centre left & centre right), back cover.

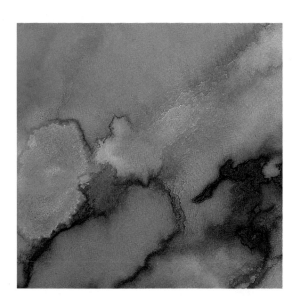

ACKNOWLEDGEMENTS

We gratefully thank the following people for their contributions in writing this book.

Our gratitude to the many staff and crew (former employees and current VIA personnel) at VIA Rail Canada who shared their expertise and personal histories of the rails. Their names are too numerous to be listed individually, but we wholeheartedly thank each and every one.

A special thanks to the English Department of the University of British Columbia for helping locate just the right Canadian poems.

As well, this publication would not have been possible without the assistance of the following individuals and organizations: The archivists of Canadian National Railways; The Provincial Archives of British Columbia, Saskatchewan and Manitoba; the librarians and staff of the Vancouver Public Library Central Branch (History, Literature, the Northwest Room, Magazines and Historical Photographs departments); Vancouver Island Regional Library, Duncan, British Columbia; and the Portage Plains Regional Library, Portage la Prairie, Manitoba.

Thanks also to the convention and visitor bureaus and/or chambers of commerce of the many municipalities, large and small, along the various routes, including but not limited to: Newmarket; Barrie; Orillia; Longlac; Holden; Evergreen Country (Edson); Lakeland; Jasper; and McBride.

MLD Publications Inc.
Publisher/Editor: Marilynne Prupas
Writer: Shauna McGovern
Production: David Favrholdt

Design & Art Direction: Jacob Benaroch
Benaroch Graphic Communication

VIA Rail Canada Inc.
P.O. Box 8116, Station A, Montréal, Québec H3C 3N3